DIVING FOR
PEARLS

A Nick Hern Book

Diving for Pearls first published in 1989 by
Nick Hern Books, a division of Walker Books Ltd,
87 Vauxhall Walk, London SE11 5HJ
Copyright © Howard Brenton 1989

British Library Cataloguing in Publication Data
Brenton, Howard, *1942–*
I. Title
823'914 [F]
ISBN 1-85459-C25-1

Typeset by Book Ens, Saffron Walden, Essex
Printed and bound by Billings of Worcester

DIVING FOR
PEARLS

A NOVEL BY

HOWARD BRENTON

N H B NICK HERN BOOKS

A DIVISION OF WALKER BOOKS LIMITED

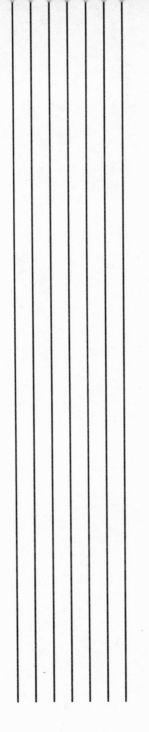

To
Ritsaert ten Cate

Who has not sat, afraid,
before the heart's curtain?

RILKE

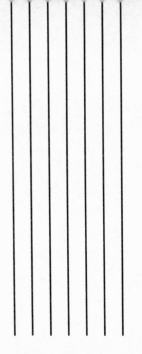

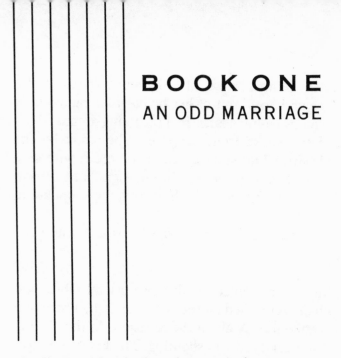

BOOK ONE
AN ODD MARRIAGE

Cecily Rose knew that she was in love.

She stared at the sweet williams in the flower border outside the open prison. The border's edge was marked by stones, painted white. Each flower was perfect. She knew they had been planted out by the prisoners, from the prison nursery, twenty-four hours before. The flowers were turned towards her with meaningless smiles.

She paused. In the unexpected warmth of a fine day at the end of a disappointing summer, she felt a little sweat in the small of her back above the waistline of her skirt. It made her skin prickle. The loose silk of her blouse was sticking. She knew she wouldn't take the jacket of her pale blue suit off, not until she was in the visiting room, and that, even then, she may not dare.

She panicked. She couldn't breathe.

She had visited many prisons, including this one, many times. She had stood in the flat Sussex landscape, by the mesh wire gate, on the first Wednesday of every month for three years now. But there was always, for a second,

1

this moment of airlessness, of a tightened throat, and a flash of seeing herself out of her body, standing alone in the anonymous country lane. In a recurring dream which she could not shake from her sleep, she stood by the flowerbed with white stones, before the mesh wire gate and the black and white board with its sign 'H.M. Prison Fordbridge', quite naked, with her arms limp, unable to move.

She breathed again and walked toward the gate, quickly.

The visiting room clanged with noise. Metal tables and tubular chairs screeched on the concrete floor. There was a feverish and false joy about the occasion. As the visiting hour wore on voices rose to shouting. The Prison Officers walked amongst the tables with bucolic smiles and the odd quip to the visitors, most of whom were women. It was cheery-time and chaffing, a fake bonhomie to cover both the tedium of the visiting hour and the wretchedness of the predicament of everyone in the room. The babble pressed on the back of her neck, her vertebrae picking up fragments of conversations, the splinters of other people's lives, as if her body were a radio antenna picking up all the woes of the world.

'What do you mean your mother said?' . . . 'Dad just goes on and on about digging the garden.' . . . 'All Mum said was, that school's got it in for the kid.' . . . 'But I keep on telling him, Dad we ain't got no garden.' . . . 'What d'you mean, that school's got it in for him?' . . . 'Did they let you have the vests?' . . . 'Yeah yeah, I got the vests.' . . . 'If he wants a garden get him a window box or something, from Woollies.' . . . 'They're tremendous vests, Doll, don't get me wrong, it's just bloody hot in here.' . . .

It was always like this. Everything was hard-edged in

the prison world, everything grated, the colour of the walls, the strip lighting that blazed from the ceiling even though sunshine poured through the windows, the cauliflower smell with a hint of excrement, the awkward angle of a visitor's hip in a cream skirt that was too tight for her, the smile on a screw's lips, his watery eyes unreadable. Everything was arranged, she thought, to give difficulty. It was the low-level torment of an exquisitely judged ugliness.

'I know what this is. This is your Mother, bitching about my kid.' . . . 'Can't you get the Council in for your Dad?' . . . 'Another thing. Shirley's gone funny about her hair.' . . . 'What? Shovel him away? Have the dustman cart him off to some home?' . . . 'She's shaved half of it off.' . . . 'Poor old Dad, no life at all.' . . . 'What do you mean, she's shaved half her hair off? She's only fourteen.' . . .

And then, for Cecily, everyone else in the room was in a dumbshow. Their mouths moved, they gestured, smiled, sweated on their foreheads, frowned, looked down or away in silence as if they were behind thick plate glass.

'You got me into this,' said Frank.

She looked at his big hand, lying loose on the grey table top. Her nails, varnished a pearl pink, were an inch from his. Before Frank, she had never painted her nails.

'Before Frank' was her phrase for so many things, ways of behaving and thinking, 'before Frank and I . . .'

Suddenly she was overcome with a sense of heaviness. Her hand was leaden. She felt her lips hang, parted by their weight. Sitting on the hard chair in her well-cut and expensive clothes, the sky-blue suit, the cream silk blouse, the armour of respectability, she was overcome by a sumptuous weariness. She was an active, aggressive woman to those who knew her, and she valued the people she knew and what they thought of her. But here she was, sweating, feeling her breasts pull apart with their weight. She wanted to let her body sag, to let all strength go, to be sprawled on a sofa in a shuttered room, legs and arms loosely akimbo, looking at a closed door, waiting. Staring at the doorknob, waiting for it to turn. It was shameful. Pull yourself together woman. You are sitting in a prison. On a hard chair. Helplessly in love.

'Helplessly . . .'

She had been warned. 'Of romantic attachments, Miss Rose', the pert and progressive wife of a dull local vicar had said at the Penal Reform Society training session, pausing with an acid look, 'all criminals are manipulative. They will seek to entangle you in their lives, helplessly.'

An acid look. 'Helplessly . . .' Cecily remembered the woman's glance. Being so improbably in love, so much against all her good sense, made her vulnerable. Even little flicks of sexual jealousy remembered from the past, like that vicar's wife's glance, were bitter sleights that burnt her with shame.

'If anything of that ilk gets under way, stop the visits at once. It is the attraction of the unattainable. Some marry when the prisoner is released. Such marriages are always, always a disaster, Miss Rose. They are truly made in hell.'

Hard words, harsh good sense from the bedrock of society's collective wisdom about human nature. She'd heard policemen, Prison Officers, Prison Governors all talk that way. Once a con, always a con. The bent stay bent. She was flying in the face of that stern, implacable wisdom and she knew it.

She shook her head.

'You got me into this,' Frank was saying. 'I put it down to you. I want you to know that.'

He twitched an elbow. His right eyelid trembled for a

4

moment. The sensitivity of a big man, Cecily thought. He hates himself for it.

'I'm fucking telling you, Cis, this is down to you.'

'Frank I will not be sworn at.'

She was as angry as he. But it was all right. It was a ritual, it was part of the strength between them. The strength against the world's wisdom.

She hissed back at him. 'So fuck you, Mr. Criminal. Mr. Gaolbird, cheap hoodlum . . .'

'Sorry . . .'

'Cheap hoodlum, cut-price Al Capone . . .'

She loved not letting him get away with a thing, not an inch, not an insult, not for a second. 'Yob. Working-class yoik.'

'Did I say sorry? I think I did say sorry.'

He paused. No don't fall silent, she thought. It's so difficult being silent together in here. Later we'll have that, when . . . He withdrew his hand and leant forward upon his elbows, speaking with a curl upon his lips. No Frank, don't do that. It was the tone she disliked. Badgering, tinpot, wheedling, she knew it came from being in prison. It was a weapon, an edge of self-pity used to accuse her. All criminals are manipulative, once a con . . .

'So sorry, right? But I tell you. In here you get a fever. Like having 'flu, all the time, it burns you up. What burns me up is I really needed that result.'

'Frank, it is a very good result.'

'A "C" for GCSE Greek?'

'And a "B" for Latin. And an "A" for English.'

'What's an "A" for English? We all fucking talk it, what's so fucking great about that?'

Frank's discovery that he could study was full of such hope that it frightened her. It was proof of her belief that human nature could change, that we could change ourselves, a belief she had clung to from her left-wing days. She saw Frank's natural and effortless literacy as a window opening on a broad landscape of freedom. 'I am the Kraken,' he'd say. 'I wake.' But it irritated her, she thought it an affectation when he spoke of his academic success as a 'result', prison slang for a sentence quashed, an appeal won.

Won perhaps by any means? A juror bribed, a bent lawyer, a witness warned off. . . . Or a dappy, 'do-gooder' middle-class Prison Visitor in her early thirties, fooled and abused?

Sometimes, from a holiday memory, she thought she was swimming under water, the metallic taste of scuba air in her mouth, trying to control her panic by slow deliberate movements as she looked down at dark rocks on the sea-floor where the fears slid amongst strange shapes.

'It's a fantastic achievement, Frank. In your . . .', she tried to bite back the words, but too late, '. . . your state.'

His anger slapped into her face.

'And what state is that then?'

'Frank, don't start . . .'

'State of a no-hoper? State of dregdom, that state?'

'Don't.'

'Oh Miss Prison Visitor. "Lift yourself up," you have said. "Attain." "Get up the mountain, survey wonders." Nah.' He leant back, waving her away. His chair screeched on the floor. Oh block out the noise for a moment longer she thought, please . . .

He flashed back at her. 'Am I just a hobby to you? At your supper parties, over the . . . What? Duck? Pheasant? Fucking peacock on the silver plate? Nah, duck, have it all the time your lot don't you, the skin o' your kind, made o' duck meat . . .'

6

Don't give him an inch . . . 'Frank, you enjoy this too much . . .'

'Over the wine glasses, "Ho ho you know what ho, I've got a little con, a-learnin' of Latin and Greek, tally ho." '

He crashed forward on his chair, his face close to her, just as a Prison Officer turned away. He clenched his fist between them.

'Three years. For a bloody "C" and a "B".'

Not for a second . . . And she was angry now. 'Yes three years! Of my life too you know. People laugh at me.'

'What do you think they do to me in here, banged up reading fucking Cicero?'

The Prison Officer turned back and Frank was, at once, sitting back on his chair. He smiled.

'No, I look after myself, I promise you. Any nonsense and . . .'.

His hand fell onto the table.

'The bastard gets divided into three parts, eh?'

Smiles. She looked down. Hands on a grimy grey table. She wanted to look up, into his face. But the heaviness, the weariness . . . And her concentration broke. The room roared again.

'And what about your socks?' . . . 'I found Dad at night, in the living room. He was digging up the carpet.' . . . 'Why do we have to talk about vests 'n' socks for an hour?' . . . 'Them teachers. Lesbians are they?' . . . 'I can't take the vests back to Mum.' . . . 'Chuck 'em out the train window on the way back then.' . . . 'He said he was digging up the carpet to plant roses. He wanted 'em to grow up over the telly.' . . . 'Have to get the Council in then.' . . . 'But they'll take him away to one of them places, they're disgusting.' . . . 'My life's in ruins and we talk about socks.' . . . 'Well you'll have to watch the telly through a load o' rose bushes, won't you?' . . .

'Show me then,' said Frank, against the babble. She lip-read what he said, the noise was so great.

Show him.

The other people in the room went back into dumbshow. There was a silence between them in the thick, hot air.

'You are this time, aren't you. So show me.'

He had asked her again and again to come on a visit not wearing a bra. Until today she had refused. She knew she would accede to his request in the end. Each time she left her Kensington flat to drive down to Sussex, she would delay dressing until the last moment. 'This silly thing he wants . . .', she'd say, 'silly . . .'. And usually she would shrug with annoyance and put on her bra, the cream silk blouse and one of her three woman's suits, to look like a businesswoman, as the Penal Reform Society advised, then leave the flat quickly without further thought. In the prison's visiting room she would always notice his glance at her breasts to see if, at last, she had given in, and he would say, just once, 'Next time, show me?' Silly, silly thing . . .

They had never kissed, but the rise and fall of their conversations, her determined steering of Frank through GCSE courses and examinations, the ritual rows, the tendernesses, the little illegal things she did for him, the passing of tobacco and chocolate, the odd five pound note screwed tight and pressed into a wad of silver foil, had caught them in a complicity that was at first a flirtation, then a courtship and finally a declaration of love. Over three years they ebbed and flowed, loved and hated, became bored, rowed and made up with the regular tidal patterns of lovers who had become used to each other. Yet all they did was sit on two hard chairs, facing each other across a table, with an unspoken agreement between them never even to touch hands.

So for Cecily to sit before him naked beneath her blouse was a terrifying acknowledgement. It had taken on the proportions of allowing a sexual act to a man, half feared and half imagined, behind the thick red curtain of perverse desire. It was to acknowledge that she was irredeemably lost and in love against all reason. Whatever the revulsion she at times felt, she had no choice.

She slipped off her jacket. He stared.

'Breathe in.'

'I . . .'

'Do it!'

She breathed. His stare was constant. 'Oh cruel sorrow.'

Wires, drawn tight, threaded through muscle, running from her lower abdomen across her inner thighs, electric wires, if they get hot, she thought, feeling an intolerable sweetness, everything will shine through my clothes, I'll be exposed, everyone will gawp, I'll be arrested, dragged away across the floor, indecent. 'Oh cruel sorrow,' came the phrase again.

'The button.'

'Oh Frank.'

'The button.'

She undid the top button of her blouse.

'Your nipples are dark.'

She lied, she didn't know why. 'I rouged them.' And smiled. She was light, This was easy, this was nothing at all. She was controlling him. She knew the slightest movement would make him wince and cave forward, hollow chested. She could bear it and he could not. He was entangled in a cat's cradle, the strings ran from her fingers into his body.

He shook his head, slowly. 'Put your coat back on, love.'

'I don't care,' she whispered.

'I do.' He grimaced then suddenly laughed, glancing about the room.

She wanted to be brazen, to say something brazen. 'They can strip me, strip search me. I'd sit naked in this place for you,' she whispered.

'Yeah? Prison Visitor streaker?'

And they were giggling. Gas bubbles of giggles rose in her chest. Such relief . . . Their eyes were wet with suppressed laughter. She slipped her jacket back on. Her muscles relaxed, warm and weak. God, she thought, I don't think I'll be able to stand up.

'Do you know?' she said, the laughter gone, 'I have never seen you . . . head to toe. Except when you walk towards this table, then when you walk away.'

'It's the same for me,' he said, serious and grave with her after their laughter.

They fell silent, not looking at each other. But the dumbshow held, the other voices and other lives remained distant, blocked out from the precious moment of reverie between them. One day, she thought, we'll sit together after a meal like this, really alone together, contented with nothing to say because everything had been said and a night of lovemaking lay ahead.

'Y'know . . .'. He hesitated. 'Y'know, since the screws got onto us . . .'

Panic jabbed in her throat. 'Onto us?'

'Oh they are onto us. Nothing in here is unseen, nothing is unknown. Before every one of your visits, and after, they give me a dry bath.'

'A what?'

'They strip search me.'

'But . . . The money . . . The money I've given you.'

'Oh I hide that. There are ways.'

'This is outrageous, I'll make a complaint to the Governor . . .'

'You don't get the point.' He leant forward. 'Each time you come, each month, for your visit, I stand the other side of that door there, stark naked. Waiting for you. Get the point?'

She looked up, straight at him, steadily. 'It's not long now, Frank.'

'No.'

'Two months.'

'Nine weeks, four days. One thousand, six hundred and eighty hours.'

'You worked that out in advance!' she said, laughing again.

'I did not! I am your working-class genius, in't I? Of your very own making.'

Their hands were so close. And the bell went off. In the confusion of last shouted goodbyes, the last instructions and requests, prisoners to loved ones, the bubble of silence that had protected Frank and Cecily was blown away. She was desperately trying to think of what she had not said. There always was something, remembered too late, as she walked from the gate . . . But he was speaking, low and quickly. Oh no, not that.

'Cis. That other thing. On the outside.'

Oh no. 'I'll do that.' No, no.

'You've got it straight.'

'Yes.'

'And you'll do it?'

!This weekend.'

'And you're crystal clear?'

For Frank had asked her, again and again, casually at first but then with increasing insistence, to do 'a thing' for him.

Why had she ever told him that her family was 'connected', his word. 'Got connections have you, high up?' Why had she told him that her sister was the lover of a Junior Minister in the Government? Because she wanted to gossip, about intimate things, she wanted to share news with him, as you do with lovers. And he had taken this sisterly secret and was bending it, tying it up.

He wants to get a message to my sister's lover. Fine. The message was just a name, an English name, bland and meaningless, Peter Carter.

This name was to be said, 'on the outside' . . . And Frank seemed certain the world would change.

Crime, manipulation, tangled complexity, she felt it pull at her private world, her family. A thread from Frank's underground, secret life was tied to it, it was pulling her into a maze.

It's a test, she thought. Will I sell my family out for this man?

'Yes,' she said angrily. 'I'll do it. I have no shame.'

He grinned. 'I know you don't.' He looked at her breasts. 'Why do we torment ourselves?'

'Because we are in torment my darling,' she said, the phrase ringing hollow to her, her face flushed, her composure gone.

The bell jangled again above the din of goodbyes. 'That's it, loves and lasses!' called a fat Prison Officer, cheerfully. 'Time, time please, ladies, gentlemen!'

'One thousand six hundred and . . . seven hours and thirty minutes, actually,' said Frank, as he stood to walk away.

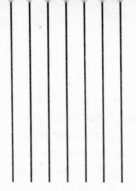

The swan flew very fast along the river, parallel to the banks, ten feet above the surface of the water in a straight line, the ferocious power of its wings sawing the air with a rasping sound.

Doleful sound, sad sound . . . Sir Stephen Rose lay back on the embroidered cushions of the punt. After the dismal days of a grey and rainy July, August was hot and sunny. It was becoming a wonderful late summer. Perhaps, thought Sir Stephen idly, all this talk of a greenhouse effect will bring to England a Mediterranean climate for my last years on earth. Which would be pleasant, the skin of young women brown beneath cotton, breakfast in the open air, wine each day in the noon heat, the wretched soddenness of this country dried out. As for skin cancer, ecological disaster, won't be here to see it, will I? Sod 'em, let the young sort it out. I have done too much for the young in my life anyway. Have I? Idleness, idly thought. Ah, on the river. One thing if England heated up. Could transform the English character, spice the dull buggers with a touch of Latin violence. which, God knows, it could do with. Witness Henry.

Henry, the husband of Sir Stephen's elder daughter, was labouring at the punt pole and talking. Sir Stephen didn't bother to listen. Henry's conversation was invariably on the subject of money and achievement, principally his own. He would even lecture sixth forms of minor public schools on 'My success'. What bored Sir Stephen was that

13

Henry really was successful and he really was honest. He associated with the robber barons of the Margaret Thatcher era, he negotiated his way with a fresh and honest face through the archipelago of companies they ran, companies which seemed to make nothing but money, and sometimes not even that. 'A fresh and honest face', that was all there was of Henry. His business associates would have their telephones tapped by the Fraud Squad and even sometimes one of them would appear on the television news, being hurried through crowds outside a court, a fat back in a sleek suit stepping ruined into the rear of a Daimler. But Henry was never there, Henry was never involved. He had 'smelt a rat' months before and 'got out'. It was a great disappointment. Sir Stephen had had high hopes that his son-in-law was a crook. As a student of human behaviour he had looked forward to the insights such a member of the family would bring. But no. He had given his eldest daughter away to a man who was simply honest and simply a bore.

Ah, a son-in-law, thought Sir Stephen, to whom I could show the books. In his library, in the biggest room on the ground floor of the house, Sir Stephen kept his library and within the library, hidden by a locked sliding panel, behind his innocuous collection of Greek and Latin texts and commentaries, a collection of pornography. He had started the secret collection in his twenties. There were privately printed volumes that had once graced, 'disgracefully graced', he smiled to himself, a nineteenth-century brothel. He had a rare Byzantine manuscript which he had bought in Damascus at the end of the war, from the last century of that mystically tormented and tormenting Empire, a book of tortures and ecstasy. He would look at it once a year, on New Year's Eve. For the other three hundred and sixty-four days it would radiate its doleful, unseen presence into the room, through the scholarly edited texts of Aeschylus and Euripides, Plato and Herodotus, Virgil and Aquinas, and a rare edition of Descartes in the original Latin. It reminded Sir Stephen of the reality that radiated behind reason, behind the great tapestry of history and culture. Had not Sir Isaac Newton, the great rationalist, the scourge of superstition, the grave digger of the last vestiges of Medievalism, written secret books of Alchemy madder, intellectually more obscene, than anything purchasable in the occult bookshops off St. Martin's Lane? When he took down, say, Descartes's 'Discourse on the Method of Rightly Conducting the Reason' from the magnificent thirteen-volume Adam and Tannery edition, published in Paris in the 1890s, he knew that behind the shelf, at that very place, there lay within the wall Lely's 'Oeuvres Complètes' of the Marquis de Sade. Behind reason, unreason. Behind pleasure, disgust. And beyond unreason and disgust, our reality.

Sir Stephen saw the swan a hundred yards off, coming toward Henry's back, its neck straight, a bolt from a crossbow, a fighter jet, its profile compact, head on . . . And waited.

He had come to terms with his misanthropy many years before. He remembered the struggle that it used to be to like people, to apply virtues to colleagues and friends when there were no virtues there, none at all, just cellulose, vibrating membranes. He remembered the relief when he acknowledged that humanity was not, really, for him. He discovered that people like Henry did not have to be either tolerated or detested, just ignored. The more you ignored the Henrys of this world, he found, the more they assumed that you valued them, that they were in your confidence, that your friendship and your advice were among the finest things in their lives. You had to do nothing to deceive the people around you, nothing at all. They did it all for themselves, trapped in the individual envelopes of their limited perceptions, the small membraned bags they called 'my personality', that trembled with their secret ambitions and puny masturbatory desires. Aie, aie, thought Sir Stephen, wearily.

The swan was fifty yards off. Henry tugged at the punt pole. 'Blaa blaa,' went his mouth.

A moment, held frozen, before violence. Sir Stephen remembered how, before an explosion, a second before, you knew it was going to happen. The next second of the future warned the present. And you understood the world, you knew what you were, standing on the planet. You were, briefly, truly alive. He had had the experience in Palestine in 1947, as a British Army Intelligence Officer. A bomb in Jerusalem, in the Old City, an Arab shop disintegrated without warning. By a freak the blast ricocheted either side of him, against the walls of the narrow street, barely brushing his clothes, and he stood there, stone deaf but untouched, while the dead and screaming lay round about him.

Palestine . . . 'Over the sea, in the tomb where Jesus lay . . .' So many years ago.

It had taken three months for his hearing to recover. To this day, his right ear was only fifty percent effective and sometimes, when he was tired, or had been drinking too much in the Cambridge College Common Room that was now his fiefdom, he would suffer from a squeaky, ringing sound, faint and eerily distant, as if the roof of his skull was as high as a cathedral and an animal was trapped, up there amongst the curving masonry, and was screaming for help.

'Help!'

The swan was at Henry's head.

But had Henry cried help? Sir Stephen had the impression the words 'Pension fund' were on his lips as the rasp of the swan's wings, with a down draft of unexpected force, surprised Henry from behind, six feet above his head.

'Pension fund!' Henry made the mistake of trying to steady himself on the pole. The pole slid on the river bed. Henry tried to balance on one foot, the other stuck out at right angles.

Pension fund? And, with Henry, leg stuck out, hand on the slipping pole, Sir Stephen had only to shift his weight with the smoothly judged timing of a cricketer glancing a ball fine off square leg, to rock the punt and send Henry falling backwards into the water.

For a blissful moment, Henry entirely disappeared beneath the surface.

I will, I suppose, one day be senile and really vicious, Sir Stephen thought, calmly.

'Marry him? You are going to marry your convict?' Matty said to her sister.

And the swan tore along its line above the river at the bottom of the garden, the expanse of the lawn tilting down to the water's edge like a great stage, the willow trees at either side forming huge curtains that framed the river view. Matty turned at the sound of the wings.

'The swans are still here,' Cis said, for something to say.

'Oh the swans . . . swan about.' Our father's swans, Matty thought, bitterly. The great heavy beauties with disgusting habits. Daddy's untamable pets.

And Cecily thought, here we are upon my father's lawn. And we are wearing floppy summer hats, with bows, as if we were Edwardians. Edwardian girls in pale pink and white chiffon, white shoes on blazing green grass, only for him. She turned, squinting in the sunlight at the large ugly Victorian house, its big windows dark, and not catching the light. Oh Matty, you shouldn't live here, you and Henry, in father's house. He has stabled you here, you are just useful animals to him. He has put you and Henry in stalls, he feeds you hay, he pats your rumps, he bridles you. You should get away from this awful house with its beautiful garden. But no, Henry thinks it will come to him when our father dies, though he has no reason to do so, no breath of a promise, let alone the sight of a will. Our father's will! What a document that will be, what a drama when it is read, what a tyrannical decree from the grave to enslave us all . . .

'When?'

The windows of the house, eyeless sockets. The grey stonework, sick flesh. 'The leprous house . . .' What poem was that from?

'Cis! Listen to me!' Matty was angry, it was all so unfair, unfair. 'When are you going to marry this jerk?'

Cecily turned to her.

'The day he is released.'

'And when is that?'

'Nine weeks, one day.' And twenty-one hours, she said to herself, warm and strong in the outrage of her new life, feeling so much younger than her sister.

'Does Daddy know?'

'Why should I tell Daddy?'

'Well! Oh come on! Daddy's got friends.'

Oh yes, Daddy has got friends, Cecily thought 'Connections.' In the University, in Government, Daddy could be Master of the College, come on Matty, Daddy will laugh, it's you and Henry you're worried for . . .

A worrier. Matty the matronly and good sister, the sunny simple one, while I'm the . . . What? Slut, the slut. But Matty was, she realised with a twinge of panic, becoming a moan. She carped, she was getting worn down. Matty, cheerful and practical for so many years, could become a scold in middle age, garrulous and complaining, her loveliness fretted away. Oh Matty, don't be sad . . .

'Don't you think Daddy should be told he's going to have a criminal in the family? God Almighty Cis . . .'

'Daddy will take a broad view, I know. Our father is a philosopher, after all. Actually you know he'll love it. He'll invite Frank to dine on high table at College, I bet you. I can see it now.'

'So can I'.

Unfair, thought Matty. Always people being so bloody unfair. Deliberately difficult . . . Oh this family and this life, thought Matty, her discontent weighing her down, a huge amorphous mass of hundreds of things . . . Henry and Daddy, the house, and now this stupidity. Cis is just like him, just like Daddy. So difficult and . . . wanton.

'It's you and Henry you're worrying about.'

No I'm not, thought Matty. No, yes I am. How can she accuse me of being selfish? Is that what she's doing?

'All right. Why not? Henry's working for Conservative Central Office for God's sake! He could be Vice-Chairman in the Autumn.'

'Matty what on earth does that have to do with my marrying Frank?'

'Oh don't play the innocent, please.' Innocent sister, with youthful looks still on her. Matty loved her so sharply she sometimes wanted to slap her face, like they did when they were children, in a sudden spat. Once, she took Cissy's dolls away and locked them up in a cupboard

19

in the pantry, then started to cry and felt horrible. This mish-mash, the contrariness of sibling love and hate, will it go on forever until we are old, old women, facing each other in armchairs in a nursing home? Yes, it will. She let her temper flare. 'You know what I mean, little sister. "Tory Big-wig's Convict Brother-in-law"? You could end up in the Daily Mail. Oh God, in the Sun, you are so irresponsible, Cis, so . . .'

Oh Matty my dear, Cecily thought, there's no way out. I am going to do terrible things to you because of me and Frank. And I see no way out.

"Course I'll tell Daddy.'

Two women on a lawn, in pretty dresses, Cecily felt that whichever way they turned, they were caught in a picture, that whatever positions they took up they were posed deliberately, caught in a visual scheme arranged by an unscrupulous photographer and from which they could not escape. Fate, the great photographer . . .

'I'll tell him now.'

'Oh no you won't. You will not mess up this weekend. Henry wants Daddy to do something. He's been working on him for weeks . . .' She looked away at the river. 'I just hope Daddy's noticed . . .'

'Working on what?'

'How do I know? Something to do with money. Or the College, the Party, the world, white slavery, outer space, I don't know! I just want, for once, Daddy not . . .'

'Not to play the cynical old fart?' said Cecily. She was disturbed by the unhappiness from Matty, the sarcastic edge, so untypical of her. She knew she must invoke the old sense of conspiracy with her elder sister, of shared secrets, torches under the bedclothes at night, Matty my big sister putting lipstick on my mouth when I was seven and she was fourteen.

'There are other people's lives going on, Cis. Around you, in your . . . bubble.'

Cecily hesitated. How could she make her sister understand, how could she make her taste a little of the intolerable sweetness that had overwhelmed her? She wanted to pimp her feeling for this man to her sister, to share him with her, just for a minute, just for an hour, so Matty would become one with them, a trusted fellow conspirator in their love. 'I know it's crazy,' she said, 'but Frank and I have never touched.'

Matty's face hardened. 'No?'

'Nor held hands. Nor kissed. It's love with a Martian. I slip him tobacco.'

Matty was about to interrupt, but Cecily pressed on. 'I slip him tobacco. Capstan full-strength. You give him a cigarette, he slits it with his thumbnail under the table. They keep a thumbnail long, to do it. Then he puts the tobacco, as dust, in his pockets so he can roll it, later.'

Look at me with sorrow, or pity, or contempt. With something on your face, please. She paused.

'I need your love, Matty.'

But Matty wouldn't meet her sister's eye. She shook her head. This is a tunnel, she thought. It goes down and down, I know what you want, sister, you want to take me with you. On an endless helter-skelter, down and down. They'll be no stopping the fall.

'Why does the do-gooder in this family always end up doing bad?' she said, wanting to hurt.

Cecily went cold. 'You may think it insane,' she said, 'but I want his baby.'

Matty flushed with anger. 'No. Oh no, not hard, hard-edged, cut-glass Cecily. Not you. After all the shouting at dinner parties you inflicted on us. After the ruined Christmases . . .'

'Matty I . . .'

'God! I remember that Christmas when you told Daddy you were a lesbian . . . What happened to all that, by the way? Wear off did it, with all the other passions, the other causes, Anti-Apartheid and C.N.D. and the Angola Freedom Committee? Was it Angola?'

'Namibia.' I have tried to do good, Cecily thought to herself. Just simply to do good. And she's right, I have behaved like an insufferable prig. Oh Matty, she wanted to say, and touch her sister gently on the arm. But Matty was in full flow.

'That Christmas, when you explained to the vicar and his carol singers that God had a cunt and the Virgin Mary had a cock . . .'

It was good she was angry. Good. 'Go on, go on, I deserve your scorn . . .'

'And after all that, now Cecily is going to get married. Like the rest of us. Big deal.'

'I'm thirty-two. I'm broody. Why deny it?'

'Shock horror! From you, "natural" behaviour? How old is he, this Frank?'

Cecily shrugged. Get it all out, Matty, squeeze it all out, you must. 'He's forty-six.'

'Figures. You know, Cis, that for once you are being typical? The woman in her early thirties, fancying a bit of marinated beef? Fine, why not? But Cecily must go one better. In her baby-lusting thirties, does she pick up some nice, Volvo-driving divorcee? Or some Polytechnic lecturer, with gentle eyes and two kids from a previous marriage? Oh no. That is too typical. Too ordinary. She has to do it through prison bars, with some animal in a cage.'

They were both upset, turned away from each other, Cecily with her eyes stinging in the light and the heat, Matty taking short breaths, overcome by her anger.

'My wild days are over, Matty. They really are.'

Matty scoffed. 'I don't believe that, not for a second.'

Wild days, renegade days, thought Cecily. My mid-twenties, when I woke up.

Renegade. Lovely word. Like a banner. 'A renegade from my class.' The romance of it.

A season with the crazies, the utopians, the 'Change the Worlders'.

She had had an affair with a tall gangly man called Tom. He was much younger than she. Nothing but a boy, an adolescent, eighteen and freakishly brilliant, having a year out before going up to Cambridge on a scholarship, full of bile, hammering his youthful metabolism with late nights, too much drink and too much talk.

They had met outside County Hall, in the last days of the Greater London Council, before the Conservative Government disbanded it. It was a 'day of action' with the left out in force. There were floats, balloons, children in pushchairs, all kinds of groups with their banners, feminists, greens, Peckham Gay Collective, Community Resource Centres, splinter parties of the Communist fringe, in windy uncertain weather with speeches by left-wing Labour Councillors through a squeaky public address system, slogans chanted through megaphones and aggressive young men in jeans and strong boots selling the entire gaudy range of Trotskyist newspapers.

The tribes of hope, the underclass of dreamers, making a last stand for Republican England, keeping the great possibilities alive.

If she could understand, if she could bring herself to join in, to throw herself into this potpourri of great causes, of a different world struggling to articulate itself

. . . But she felt hesitant and out of place. It was all so tatty, so silly round the edges.

Cecily was working in a solicitor's office. A friend of her father, of course, Graham Pocock. 'Bumbler Pocock, he'll take you in,' her father had said. The office was rather like a set of Cambridge College rooms, comfortable, with soft leather furniture, and so were the people she worked with, comfortable, the younger partners beginning to show the first layers of fat from good lunches. She was well paid but she was really only a glorified clerk. She was bored by the bright thirty-year-old men in their good suits, with their clear skins flushed by gin and tonics on a Friday night. She deflected their polite invitations to a tennis club or the National Theatre. They were all married anyway. She resented being the first twinge of infidelity in their lives.

An anger was rising in her.

The materialism of the early eighties oppressed her. Not that that was how she put it to herself then, she could not articulate the sense of exasperation that was over-coming her. It was the surfaces of things that made her wince, a gold Rolex watch on the wrist of a twenty-four year-old, drunk in a city wine bar, or, on the television news one night, the mother of a twelve-year-old girl who had been abducted being asked by the interviewer, 'How do you feel about the man who did this?', then the tear-clotted eyes gone and news about a golf-tournament on the screen, or a racist remark by a barrister at a confer-ence in the office, 'This hopeless case, Rich Wog v. Regina', which everyone let pass, and how women were once again in high heels in the streets, with their calves stretched, put back into tight clothing after the wear-anything spirit of the 1970s . . . by something that was happening to the country that was demeaning, making everything mean, making surfaces nasty.

Then the Falklands War broke out.

Passing a pub in Sloane Square the night the
Argentinian cruiser, the Belgrano, was sunk by a British
submarine, she turned on a group of drunken young men
who were singing 'Rule Britannia' and hit one of them,
with the side of her fist, full in his face. There was a
stunned silence. She ran away from them, as the jeers
began. Back in her flat she vomited into the kitchen sink.

Recovering, a muscle in her stomach strained, she sat
alone in her living room, the lights off, with a sense of
peace inside her, a silence. The country had gone mad.
She felt she was a secret agent, though conspiring for
what foreign power or alien cause she could not say.
What am I? she thought. A one-woman insurrection? And
laughed. She felt absurd. Next morning she unplugged
her television set, with its endless news of the war in the
South Atlantic and sudden Ministry of Defence bulletins,
and dumped it in the big rubbish bin at the rear of the
building.

A gesture.

She began to hang around demonstrations, fringe
meetings of the far left, saying nothing and talking to no
one, feeling out of place and ill at ease in her good clothes.
In the Conway Hall in Red Lion Square, she heard a
speaker from the Revolutionary Communist Party, a
splinter group from the official Communist Party, speak
of the British working class with a purity and a certainty
that she could not believe but ached to. At a meeting of
the Workers Revolutionary Party in a strange hotel ball-
room in Victoria, beneath chandeliers with worn-out
white-faced teenagers in dark anoraks sitting upon gold-
painted chairs, she heard Vanessa Redgrave talk of the
conspiracy of the American banks, of the power of money

manipulated from air-conditioned heights in Manhattan and Chicago. The operatic vision of massive, unfeeling evil blighting the planet moved her. She read left-wing books and magazines, a pile of them accumulating in the corner of her bedroom. Her reading was shame-faced, like a schoolboy reading soft porn secretly, when his parents were out of the house.

At the office she fell silent. Her popularity waned. She became poker-faced and disliked. Malicious remarks began. She was frigid, she was having a secret affair with someone in the Attorney General's Office and was 'stuck up' about it. The gossips had no idea that in her handbag was a battered copy of Bakunin and the latest Republican News, which she bought each week in the Charing Cross Road.

When, at the 'Save the G.L.C.' march, she first caught sight of Tom, he was in a melee of demonstrators and abusing a policeman. Clearly the policeman was, reluctantly, about to do something about it. Cecily went up to this young man, spitting his obscenities at the agent of the state, and simply pulled him away. Tom skidded. He sported Trotskyite boots, those favoured by the Socialist Workers Party, with nails on their soles, and fell. He turned to abusing her.

And that afternoon she took him back to her flat and seduced him in two hours of disorderly, puppyish love-making, drinking cheap wine as if there were no tomorrow.

Renegade romance . . . To cheap Italian red and cans of Carlsberg Special Brew.

And, indeed, Tom and his circle were most of the time recklessly drunk. There were five or six of them, much younger than she, two of them rather frightening fifteen year-old girls from Pimlico Comprehensive.

She was always out of place with them and ill at ease.

Cradle snatching? If people knew what she was doing every other night, every weekend, with these children. . .

But she was caught up in their passionate discussions, around the coffee table of Tom's tiny Peckham bedsit piled up with unwashed plates and the stained cartons of old takeaway meals. They were childish, but fervent.

Hope, hope oh hope . . .

The group would go down of a night to join a permanent picket outside the South African Embassy, with sandwiches and Tom's thermos flask full of coffee laced with whisky. Their other activity was the painting of C.N.D. slogans on walls and pavements, late at night. This was taken very seriously. The subject of the interminable discussions over the neglected washing up was usually centred on what the slogans were to be, 'Jobs Not Bombs', 'Teachers Not Trident' . . .

Then one night they were discovered, brushes and paint tins in their hands, hair and clothes flecked with white paint, by a passing police panda car. They were defacing the front of an Army Careers Office at Camberwell Green. This time it was Tom's turn to rescue Cecily from 'the clutches of the neo-fascist state', as the group put it.

'Run!' he had shouted, and Cecily and the two schoolgirls did, dropping their brushes. Cecily looked back. Tom had stood his ground, and she saw him flailing his fists at two policemen.

First thing the next morning, after a terrible two hours in the shower getting the night's political paint out of her hair, Cecily stormed into Graham 'Bumbler' Pocock's room in the solicitor's office and lied . . . The brilliant son of a friend . . . Mixed up in this silly nonsense.

The firm were pleased that Cecily was at last talking to them again. One of their brighter sparks was given the simple little case, fees waived, a favour for Cecily's family, helping the wildly young, a story to tell in the wine bar.

She felt ashamed. Shriven. The great pussycat of influence purred for her and a paw effortlessly swept the problem under the carpet.

When the case came to court, Tom was short-haired and dressed in a new, charcoal-grey suit, with a white shirt and a tie. His South London accent had disappeared. His parents were there, a divorced couple. His father was not the British Railways porter Tom had claimed but a surgeon, with the red face of a heavy drinker that Cecily saw so often amongst barristers. He specialised in hip replacements. They thanked Cecily for her 'concern'.

The charge against Tom of assaulting a police officer was dropped. He pleaded guilty to criminal damage, was fined and bound over to keep the peace for two years. Three months later he went up to Oxford.

They had a half-hearted correspondence but the letters petered out. She never visited him.

She could not remember from all the hours of talk and passionate argument a single thing he had said, the bits and pieces of the vanguard role of the working class, borrowed from the Revolutionary Communist Party, the role of the American banks borrowed from Vanessa Redgrave, all mixed up with a kind of jejune anarchism, passed away like a light shower of rain dried from a pavement. Just the mad hope that the boy had represented for her remained, with the memory of his babyish skin pitted here and there by an adolescent boil and the roughness of a light beard about his lips.

Cecily threw out the pile of books and magazines and redecorated her flat. She bought a portable television.

She began an affair with one of the junior partners in the firm. Sutcliffe, Sutcliffe Jones.

Sutcliffe liked boats. They had weekends together in a rowdy sailing pub in Cambridgeshire on the river Ouse. The pub was a safe haven for married men on dirty weekends. That appeared to be its sole trade, and the management connived at the arrangements. Sutcliffe joked that they kept two hotel registers, one the real record of guests, the other a fiction of false names for snooping divorce lawyers. Cecily found herself drinking with the girlfriends of Sutcliffe's friends, while the men drank late into the night on one of the boats. She came to loathe herself for these trips. The dark red carpets in the pub seemed to smell of sperm as well as beer. The affair sputtered on through a winter and died. They continued to work together, in a deadpan way. Indeed, the whole affair had been deadpan. His wife never knew.

Cecily told herself she was biding her time. She began to grieve for the childish, make-believe nights of the would-be revolutionary cell. The humiliation of its debacle wrankled.

She was biding her time before breaking out again, before making another dash into the conspiracy for freedom that she knew must be there, below the surface selfishness of the city, working its purpose out in secrecy.

Then, two years later, at a Chilean Solidarity Concert at the Dominion Theatre, she bumped into one of the schoolgirls from the group, now a hardened young woman with short hair and the strained look of a serious activist. She said that Tom had given up political activity and then dropped out of university, caught up in some kind of religious cult, an off-shoot of the Church of Scientology.

Her name was Mary Winters. She was with a tall woman in her early forties, who did not speak. After the concert the three of them stood in the Dominion's foyer, awkwardly, trying to be still as the audience pushed around them. Records were being sold of the music played at the concert by the exiled Chilean band, Inti Illuminati. Cecily had resisted the emotional impact of the weird, soaring notes of the flutes, the eerily impassioned songs that wailed of the death of heroes whose names she did not know and the beauty of the High Andean snows. She felt the familiar dislocation, the contrary mixture of a desire to belong and an inability to do so. It was too easy, she felt, to sit in a dark auditorium in a partisan crowd, the dank smell of London rain rising from winter clothing, and be moved by the laments and cries from an exotic faraway country in the grip of tyranny. The dissident thought kept coming to her—what about us? In grotty London? What are we doing about the lesser evils, the gentler oppression that afflicts us? Sod all.

'Eveline, I'd love an album,' Mary said. The tall woman smiled and moved to the scrummage at the trestle table where they were being sold. Mary looked directly at Cecily, who understood at once. They were lovers.

They went for a drink in an ugly, crowded pub in Oxford Street. Pop music thumped the back of the neck. Mary and Eveline drank Perrier water. 'Here, I bought you one,' Eveline said suddenly to Cecily and held out a copy of the Inti Illuminati record. On the rather old-fashioned sleeve the Andes soared in technicolour.

Cecily was embarrassed. 'Thank you,' she said and blushed.

A young male drinker who was pressed up against her with his companions, made a farting noise through bulbous red lips. Cecily glared at him. 'No offence, talkin' to my mate darling,' he said.

'Let's get out of here,' said Eveline.

On the pavement outside the pub they hesitated in the rain. 'Come back with us,' Mary said.

'No, I'm tired,' Eveline said, with finality, but smiled. 'Tomorrow for tea.' She gave an address in Wandsworth.

And Cecily entered the difficult world of the two women.

Mary and Eveline craved stability and, for the first few meetings with Cecily, gave the impression that their life together was, indeed, certain and resolved. The Wandsworth house where they shared a flat was in a backstreet terrace. It was one of the innumerable, unexceptional roads of the London hinterland, tree-lined and permanently parked up with cars, the privet hedges wildly overgrown, big black rubber dustbins at the gates.

'An old man was found dead last Christmas, in that house, over there,' said Eveline one afternoon, when they were looking out of the windows in the front room of the flat. 'He'd been dead for weeks. What was strange was that there was a cup, upside down in a saucer. And there were maggots, inside the cup.'

Eveline's view of the world was remorseless.

Nothing said, done, no item of clothing worn, no gesture, failed to carry a hidden meaning for her. Everything was evidence of an all-pervasive contamination of life, language and thought. The first impression of a silent woman was quite wrong. Cecily found that once you were in Eveline's circle she talked all the time and always analytically. Thus the dead man in the house over the way was not a sad, tragic incident, but 'a consequence'. His death was the death of community, the nuclear family, the heterosexual world disposing of an old man's unneeded genes. He was also a victim of his own male arrogance, too proud to seek out a neighbour and break his loneliness.

'You mean it was not his fault and was his fault at the same time?' Cecily argued.

'It's acquiescence,' Eveline smiled. 'Women are caught by it all the time.'

You could not win, Cecily found, with Eveline. You ended up nodding with a sheepish grin, grunting 'Yeah, yeah', as she soared into an argument like a manic electric guitar player. The only hope was to say nothing, so as not to set her off on another musical riff, a technique that rarely worked, because to Eveline everything connected to everything else. In a queue of women at the post office collecting children's benefit, toddlers miserable in pushchairs and the male teller sullen and bad tempered, Eveline saw an image from the Warsaw Ghetto of women standing in a line for bread, their ankles swollen.

'Oh come on, Eveline! You can't compare!'

'It's not a comparison, it's an echo. In peace or war, it's the women who queue for bread.'

In the insult shouted by a drunk one night as the three of them walked to the flat, she heard the cry of a child, molested and murdered in a wood. 'Eveline, come on! Not all men . . .'

'All right, Cis. Go over and smile at him. Now.'

'Don't be absurd . . .'

'Go over to the man, invite him in for a cup of coffee to sober up.'

'Eveline!'

'You daren't.'

'I don't want to.'

'You daren't.

'All right, I don't dare!'

'No. And we know why.'

Infuriating Eveline, tall, thin, long faced, slightly

stooped, but always consciously trying to sit upright, her fair hair cut short, her hands long, the fingers often slightly trembling, about her a waft of garlic, for she believed in the efficacy of garlic pills.

Dazzling Eveline, who wanted to live perfectly, by her lights as she saw it. 'Live by your lights', a phrase she loved. Who tried to marry mind and deed. To whom 'lifestyle' was not a collection of objects from the colour supplements, but something you crafted, delicately, a kite you made from fragile paper and balsa wood, painted with symbols of freedom, and flew.

Practical Eveline, on Tuesday, Wednesday and Friday nights on duty at a Clapham women's refuge, unpaid, and on Monday nights, counselling runaway thirteen year-olds at Euston station for a Woman's Action Group of no official standing and itself subjected to as much police harassment as those it sought to help.

Militant Eveline, on every march and picket announced in the feminist press, off to the Greenham Common Peace Camp with a present for the women there of cakes baked in her and Mary's small Belling oven.

Disruptive Eveline, pain-in-the-neck heckler of male platforms at left-wing public meetings, feared at Wandsworth Town Hall, to the door of which she chained herself when the Council refused to give the South London Prostitutes Collective a grant.

Generous Eveline, putting people up in the small backroom or on the kitchen floor of the flat, waif teenagers saved from the touting pimps of Euston station, or desperate cases who'd turned up to the Women's Refuge and found it already full.

Self-mocking Eveline, who could, flushed with anger after one of her riffs, laugh and say, 'I know I am a parody of myself.'

Vulnerable Eveline.

Beside the raging furnace of her partner's personality, Mary stood quietly, calm in the glow. She was always there, but self-contained, distant. In the days of the slogan painting cell, she had been talkative and outgoing, even, though Cecily kept the word to herself, 'sluttish'. She remembered the wild schoolgirl, naked but for her panties, leaning on her elbows on Tom's messy coffee table, drunk with a can of Special Brew in her hand. Now she was always modest, haughty and did not drink alcohol at all. Mary and Eveline never seemed to confer, they were complete in their assurance of each other. They simply looked at you together. Sometimes they would hold hands, gravely, but never in public. It was not that they were secret about their love affair. It was a 'given', it was assumed.

For a while Cecily thought the asceticism of the flat was because of Eveline's fastidiousness. She had made the double bed in the front room herself, from cheap deal. Pale brown cushions on the duvet made it serve as a couch. There were no pictures on the walls, Cecily assumed because the ramifications of meaning given off by any reproduction of a famous painting would be intolerable for Eveline. There were only two decorations. One was a beautiful narrow strip of woven silk five feet long, with horizontal bands of colour that went through the spectrum layer on layer. The other, shockingly out of place in this feminist household, was a huge fluffy ostrich feather, dyed pink, that screamed of striptease, of a cheap show in a Soho club. Cecily never mentioned the feather. It hung like a blatant talisman in the otherwise severe room of pale thin rugs, paperback books ranged in a line around the wainscot, a cheap cassette player on the floor, music tapes neatly stacked in a rack ingeniously made

AN ODD MARRIAGE

from matchboxes glued together.

But it was not from asceticism that Mary and Eveline lived so simply. It was from poverty.

Cecily learnt that the flat belonged to a woman friend of Eveline's who was in Australia, 'perhaps for a year'. Or perhaps not. Perhaps the owner would appear at any moment, with a removal van, full of the true furnishings of the flat, out of storage.

The sublet was illegal. Their 'cohabitation' was illegal, according to the Byzantine rulings of the Department of Health and Social Security. A static electricity of 'illegality' flickered around their lives.

It was Eveline's aim to 'get out of the system'. But the buff envelopes still fell on the mat, a drizzle of enquiries, demands, dates for interviews which were never kept.

Cecily was shocked to realise how poor they really were. Mary had a line in baby-sitting for two pounds an hour, amongst the local Labour Party, though Eveline was always on edge when she was out doing it. Eveline had once been a Social Worker, but had resigned, under a cloud. There was a child at risk, there was an enquiry, there was a father . . . She was never clear to Cecily about what had happened. She had an erratic income from secretarial work, as a temp amongst the Action Groups and Solidarity Committees. They fed off Eveline's constant baking, cakes and scones, wholemeal loaves, the cheaper vegetables, lentils given them from a health food co-operative, another of Eveline's causes. They had no washing machine. Eveline washed their clothes by hand in the bath, in the cramped, triangular bathroom. 'Like a woman in India at the edge of the Ganges,' she joked.

'We want a child,' Eveline said suddenly one rainy afternoon.

They were eating warm scones and strawberry jam.

Cecily had brought the jam. The rain hung on the windows in a bead curtain. Cecily hadn't noticed before that the windows were very dirty, in contrast to the immaculate, obsessive cleanliness of the flat. The windows belonged to 'out there', not the 'in here' sanctuary of the frugal living room.

'That gob-smacked you,' said Mary, unsmiling.

'But how can you adopt . . .', Cecily began. And stopped. They looked at her. 'Oh.'

'Yes, we need a man for this,' Eveline said and laughed. 'We have been discussing how to go about it.'

'Er . . . Which of you . . . ?'

'It has to be Mary,' said Eveline. 'A first child in my forties, we don't want the risk. I would be what they call an "elderly premagravid".' When Eveline said 'they' in that tone she meant 'men'. 'And we want to have the baby at home.'

'So it's me,' Mary said.

'There's a midwifery collective in Croydon, we've been out there to some meetings. They're very supportive, very loving.'

'Oh good,' said Cecily.

'Our problem is, we want what a man has got, but we don't want the man. If this were California, we could go to a sperm bank, under the counter if you get my meaning. Though Mary is dubious, even if that were possible. She feels the fucking is part of the process,' explained Eveline.

'Yes, I s'pose it is,' said Cecily.

And the three of them were laughing uncontrollably.

When they had recovered, Eveline continued. 'We want a man we don't know. Not in our circle, Trots or Labour Party.'

'Yuck,' said Mary, with a grimace.

'He mustn't know anything about us,' continued Eveline. 'We thought of a fuck on Wandsworth Common but it's too dangerous.'

'Oh?'

'Diseases.'

'Oh.'

'What we need is a married man. With an AIDS test. Perfect cover and one hundred percent secrecy. A professional guy. Fit, not too young so he won't get emotional. Not too old, so his semen will be good,' said Eveline, though it was as if the two women were talking to her in unison.

They paused. They gave her that twinned, equal, frontal stare. 'Can you help us, Cis?'

'Sutcliffe, can I buy you lunch?' she said to her dull ex-lover, in the office the next morning.

The Saturday afternoon of the weekend Mary was away with him, Cecily went round to the flat. She found Eveline drinking red wine. She was tipsy. Cecily got a cup from the kitchen and joined her. They sat cross-legged on the living room floor.

'Yes I'm jealous, what do you think?' Eveline said, straight out.

'I've not seen you drink before.'

'No. I don't. It's her. She's alcoholic. Didn't you know? I dried her out.'

Cecily saw the red carpet of the bar in the Suffolk boating pub. She had been drunk all the time when he'd taken her there. Oh God, she thought.

Mary returned, sober and quiet, and six weeks later they invited Cecily round to give the news that she was pregnant. Cecily walked to her car in the Wandsworth back street with tears streaming down her face, moved by the wild, mad joy of the two women.

Seven months into the pregnancy, at another now ritual teatime with scones and strawberry jam, Eveline said, 'We want to show you something, Cis. Say if you mind.' They left the room. A few minutes later they came back. Mary was naked.

'See?' said Eveline, curving her hand over Mary's burgeoning belly, the belly button beginning to protrude, a leaf pattern of blue veins shining on the left side of her stomach, luminous just beneath the skin.

'See?' said Eveline, cupping a hand beneath Mary's full breast, almost touching.

'See?' with a finger and thumb almost holding Mary's huge nipple, dark brown on the slight young woman's heavy breast.

'See?' and softly Eveline turned Mary sideways, and with the palm of her hand described how the small of Mary's back was hollowing inward. 'Everything is changing, she's transforming herself.'

The wonder held them. They stood silently in the room, a naked young woman late in her pregnancy, and two older women, clothed, looking at her gravely. It was as if they were taking part in a sacrament never practised before, which they were instituting for the first time.

Then Mary put her arms round Cecily's neck and kissed her, full on the mouth. Cecily felt the fulness of Mary's body hanging against hers. They laughed, Eveline hugged them, they swirled round and round the living room, cumbersomely, in a stumbling dance.

For the only time, Cecily slept with them that night. Later she was not sure whether the fluttering caresses, Mary despite her big belly as nimble as a monkey, scampering over Cecily, the cuddles, the kisses, were how Mary and Eveline usually made love. She could not tell if they were being circumspect with her so as not to frighten her away. In the morning when she woke Mary was huddled in the centre of the bed, her big belly resting on Cecily's thigh. Eveline lay apart from them, turned away, on the edge of the mattress. In her sleep she muttered a few words that were in a foreign language Cecily did not understand.

And in that bed Mary's baby, a girl, was born. Eveline telephoned the news to Cecily. She rushed round to the flat. But the room was full of women she didn't know. The Croydon Midwifery Collective? They stared at her. These people, from a whole area of Mary and Eveline's life she knew nothing about, why didn't they speak? Why wasn't she introduced to them? She felt an intense resentment, even hatred, directed at her as she held the baby, the miniature face etched in soft skin, grimly asleep. Eveline was drawn and tense.

'Is something wrong?' Cecily whispered to her, all eyes in the room upon them.

'Just tired.'

Mary, like her child, was asleep, turned to the wall. Cecily muttered congratulations and left as soon as she could. But as she opened the street door she heard Eveline call, 'Cis . . .', and she ran down the stairs to embrace her, her face wrecked with weeping.

'Oh Cis, it will be all right, won't it?'

'Yes, yes it will . . .'

'No tell me . . .'

'It will be all right. Eveline, nothing happened? With Mary, having the baby here, I mean not in hospital?' Meaning oh God, oh God, Mary and the baby, they aren't sick . . . ?

'No no. That was wonderful. Loving, and . . . strange. Strangely easy.' She hesitated, then said in a low voice, with a haunted look Cecily had never seen before, 'I'm afraid.'

Cecily moved to hold her hands, to comfort her. But above there was a thin cry. The baby had woken.

'No.' Eveline pulled away and then said, 'I held her. When she was born. Just a few minutes old. I saw her future, Cis. I know that she'll have to kill to live.' She turned to run up the stairs with a glance that burnt into Cecily's memory. It was of terror.

'Cecily, can I buy you lunch?' Sutcliffe said at the office, a few weeks later. She stared at him. He was letting his hair grow longer.

'I love her,' he said, over his Scampi Provençal at a wine bar table. 'You've got to tell me where she is.'

'No Sutcliffe. No, no no.'

'She's had a little baby girl.'

Cecily was shocked. How did he know? They're writing to each other, telephoning, they're getting to each other somehow.

'You've got to help me, Cis. You're the go-between. I mean, you were the Nurse in *Romeo and Juliet* for us.'

'You mean the pimp,' she said, bitterly. This big, fleshy man, no longer youthful, how repellent he was. Cecily thought, I am seeing him as Eveline would, his big, gingery hands, his powdery and freckled skin, his voice thick with sentimentality, an emotionally soft but power-ful man, dangerous to the secret women's world of Eveline, Mary and the child.

'She's seventeen, Sutcliffe. She's a mess, Sutcliffe. And you are thirty-five, Sutcliffe, you are married, Sutcliffe, Sutcliffe are you listening to me?'

'I don't care,' he said. 'I'll go through the fires of hell.'

'She also loves another.'

'Don't worry about that,' he said. 'I can see off that vicious old dyke, any day.'

With a sweep of her hand Cecily swept his plate of food to the tiled floor and walked out of the wine bar.

She dreaded his return to the office that afternoon. But he did not appear. Nor did he for the rest of the week. Then she heard that Sutcliffe Jones had been offered a job as a legal consultant to a Belgian firm. The office grapevine was agitated. The gossip was that Sutcliffe had knocked up some girl. And one afternoon a taut, well-dressed woman in her late thirties was shown into the senior partner's office. It was Mrs. Sutcliffe Jones, come to discuss legal matters. Sutcliffe had left her, rustled the grapevine. Cecily was paralysed as the rumours of the grand passion delighted the staff, fuelling the laughter on Friday nights over gin and tonics.

Paralysed. Six weeks went by. No word from Eveline.

Finally, one evening, she drove to Wandsworth. She sat for half an hour in the car, steeling herself. She dreaded that Eveline would accuse her of betrayal. But when she rang the bell, something was wrong. Laughter and pop music came from the first floor flat. A young man, in jeans and black tee shirt, answered the door. Student. Oh, the woman who used to live there? Miss Lacey? Yes, Eveline Lacey. Gone to Australia. An address? A shrug, a shake of the head.

Cecily felt bereaved by the disappearance of the two women. When she heard of a plane accident in some part of the world the irrational thought would come, 'Oh, I hope Eveline and Mary weren't on that plane . . .'

For only when they had vanished from her life, did she realise the influence they had had on her. She grieved for them. She blamed the loss of them on the city, how in the sprawl of London friendships are made by chance

41

encounter, then lost by accident, a telephone call not made, a postcard not sent, a visit neglected. In the blast of London traffic, the miles of terraced houses, the bedsits, the West End on rainy nights, the bleary pubs jammed with drinkers, contact could be lost, love dissipated under the assault of the city's indifference.

Massive indifference, 'the yahoo culture' Eveline called it, 'the brutish dull thump of the world they've made.' Things Eveline had said kept coming to her. 'I will show you the measure of life in a lager can and a sinkful of washing up . . .' 'What forbids us, Cis?' And, 'I know that she'll have to kill to live.' The look on her face, the last time Cecily saw her.

The image darkened with memory. Eveline was going down a staircase, not up. Towards a dark door. A cellar, a cave, and then in Cecily's dreams, a tunnel with blue walls, blue as the veins on Mary's pregnant stomach, branching into strange rooms, full of voluptuous bedding and exotic plants, their leaves feathery and unearthly in colour, like the feather that had hung on the wall of the flat.

New colours? New plants? Grown secretly, in an underground headquarters of secret desires?

Sweet words became sour, a compliment an insult, an innocuous remark an intolerable obscenity.

'And how is our Cis today?'

'I am not your Cis.'

She cultivated the crude shock. 'What's Cis up to this weekend?' asked an elderly and eminent barrister.

'Oh, I thought I'd suck some black cock. What are you up to?'

In meetings at the office she argued, she infuriated, she felt needled and needled back. She could not click out of it, her skin crawled with a thousand irritations, it was as if the professional world of the law had infested her with lice, they were burrowing into her skin. On a visit to her father, she learnt that the firm had alerted him.

'Pocock, the Senior Partner, thinks you're going potty,' laughed Sir Stephen. 'Are you?'

So she left the solicitor's office, abruptly, giving no reason. She had thought of a wrecking spree on the console of the office computer, or of setting fire to her desk, or of doing something creative with a Stanley knife to the leather sofas and armchairs, whose lumpy presence had come to represent the stolid boredom of legal work.

But she knew the time for gestures was gone, painting slogans on night walls, smashing a man's plate of food, spitting at policemen on a 'Reclaim the Night' march with Mary and Eveline. The time was gone.

She was hardening.

She went underground, within herself. She found work with a charity organisation. 'Do-gooder,' Sir Stephen had teased. But, to Cis, it was a disguise, a perfect front to do bad against a conspiratorial world. Her anger had become cunning. She took up prison visiting, using her respectable exterior. What had she told herself? She couldn't remember, because, three months into being a prison visitor, she had met Frank Blake.

And had to face the fact that her renegade instincts, her obscure and inarticulate drive to some personal insurrection, which she could not explain even to herself, were those of an incurable romantic.

Renegade, romance . . .

Oh Matty, she thought, you suspect me. You suspect I am a fraud, don't you?

Other people's ways, thought Matty. Why do I have to understand what other people are doing so well, when

43

they are blithely innocent? Am I the only one awake, forever pulling sleepwalkers away from open windows? Am I
the only one with a sense of real life at all in this family?
The ways, their ways. Her father's ways, and Henry's,
and the home-help's ways, and the builders', months
behind with the extension work on the scullery . . .

Everyone else with absolute problems, that Matty had
to be amazed at and had to help with. For everyone else
had something extraordinary going on in their lives, they
were in fabulous predicaments. But not me, never me,
thought Matty.

Even though she had been unfaithful to Henry for
three years now, that didn't count, did it? Her love affair,
which caused her great pain, was nothing. Mundane,
compared to her father's disastrous seduction of a Swiss
au pair girl less than a third of his age, or to Cecily's sexual
campaigns. That teenage boy, then those awful women
she's got involved with. And now some Don Juan of a
hairy criminal . . .

They all weakened her.

But of course she turned to Cecily, and smiled. And
held out a hand to reassure.

She was Matty. That was what Matty always did.

'I'll do what I can for you Cis, of course I will.' Of
course Matty will . . .

Cecily was flooded with relief. 'I know you will,' she
said and took her sister into her arms in a gentle embrace.

And Matty knew at once there was more.

'There is something.'

'Surprise, surprise.'

They were holding both hands between them, as if
about to swing their arms together.

'Its . . . dangerous.'

'Oh really?'

'But exciting.'

Oh well, I am Matty. She made light of it, saying, 'Hearing you say that, I catch my breath. There are prickles going up my arms.'

Now, thought Cecily. But her father was walking onto his lawn with Henry. A Henry drenched from head to foot.

'We have punted,' Sir Stephen said, with an airy wave of the hand. 'Merrily along. Ripples. Old Moley on the bank under the willows. Thank God there is still the odd weekend when you can be silly in this country.'

'You're wet,' Matty said to Henry, flatly, seeing towels, wet footprints on the carpets. And, three days on, a husband with a cold, Friar's Balsam, paracetamol and a lot of fuss.

'Cecily my dear, you got here,' said Sir Stephen, the father of largesse, his arms wide for his favourite. Matty kept her face straight.

'Hello Daddy.' Cecily hugged him then kissed him on the cheek. Large pores in his skin. A breath of tobacco, a musky aftershave. The immemorial smell of her father.

'Yes I fell in!' said Henry, enthusiastically. 'I'll nip indoors and rub down.'

'Use the blue towels in the bedroom,' Matty said to his departing back as he strode toward the house. Why oh why are fools so happy, she thought.

'Send that girl out with a drink,' Sir Stephen called after him and turned back to Cecily. 'Well, daughter mine, how are all the great causes? Injustice, the ecosphere, prison reform, battery chickens? Was it battery chickens or battered women?'

Oh no, thought Matty.

But Cecily was calm. 'The great causes go on, Daddy.'

'God rot great causes. Know who said that? Lenin.'

'Did he?'

'Where is that girl? What was her name?' Sir Stephen said to Matty.

'Tracey'.

'Tracey!' he roared at the house. 'Alcohol!'

'Where did Lenin say that?'

'Are you accusing me of fabricating a quotation?'

'Daddy,' Matty pleaded, 'please don't set her off . . .'

But Sir Stephen was away. 'Against social amelioration. Against the blurring of class conflict by works of charity. Essential Lenin.'

'But did he say it?'

'One . . .', he waved his hand again, '. . . feels that he said it.'

' "Feels"?' Cecily knew he was baiting her. She knew the glint in his eye, she saw his mind, a gyroscope spinning, turning this way and that, to find the phrase that would unbalance her. And he nearly always did.

'I know I know,' he said. 'I have taught Hegelian logic, professionally, for half my life. But in the end . . . Nah! You Utopians. For what do you agitate and why? Look about us. A lawn. Water. Sunlight. Did you see the swan's progress? An ideal world is all about us.'

He's got me, thought Cecily, anger at her throat. 'Ideal for some,' she said. 'Have you ever been in a British prison?'

'Oh no,' said Matty, aloud.

'Of course I've not been in a British prison. I have a very good accountant. Don't we Henry?' He turned. 'Where is Henry?'

'Rubbing down,' Matty said. 'Didn't you notice he was soaked?'

'Ballast!' Sir Stephen continued. 'Your criminal classes are ballast. One needs a few thousand bodies squirming in the bilges. It keeps the ship of state upright. How else can one enjoy the view from the bridge?' He was laughing now. 'Come on Cecily, explode, do. We all want you to. Not mellowing in your thirties, are you?'

But Cecily was in control of herself. She strained a grin.

'Oh my daughters,' he said, his arms wide. 'My dear girls, what joy . . . Is there drink on the way?'

And Tracey, the maid, was walking down the lawn of the house carrying a silver tray, upon it champagne in an ice bucket and glasses. She was seventeen years old. She wore jeans slit at her knees and upon each thigh, revealing thin white legs. A black tee shirt drooped with myriad badges. An orange Mohican hair style, adorned with brass studs, cleaved her shaved head.

'My God,' said Cecily, startled. And wanted to bite her tongue out.

'Do I have to stand here all day then?' Tracey said in strongest Scouse.

'Here . . .', Cecily took the tray from her.

Tracey turned to Matty. 'I think the washing in the tumble dryer's melting.'

'Then switch it off.'

'You reckon?' And Tracey strode back up the lawn to the house.

'She ran away from home,' Matty said to Cecily, irritated that she felt embarrassed. This huge house, the cleaning, the hundred and one things, who was to do them all?

'A lot of Liverpudlian maids about these days,' Sir Stephen remarked. 'The way things are going, I s'pose they're cheaper than Filipinos.'

'But don't Liverpudlians have visa problems getting into the South of England?' said Cecily.

'They cross the border at Watford illegally.' He lifted the champagne bottle.

'Hold on Cis,' Matty whispered.

'I don't know if I can.'

'Try.'

'I want to kiss him one moment and kill him the next. As usual . . .'

'You'll make it. Press your legs together, hard.'

The sisters smiled. The same things felt, the same things said, the bonding of family rituals. Whenever she visited, Cecily could not help a bright hope that this time it would be different. She, her father and her sister would coin feelings and words anew, like strangers discovering that, actually, there was love between them. She knew it wouldn't happen, of course.

Sir Stephen was twisting the champagne's cork. 'Bubbles in the afternoon sun. The glint of the passing moment and . . .'

The cork popped. He filled two glasses. 'That's for you', and he took the other two glasses from the tray and was shambling toward the house, waving the bottle. 'Going to find Henry,' he said. At the door he waved. 'Pretty hats,' he called out and was gone.

Cecily dumped the tray with its empty bucket down on the grass.

Let a cloud cross the sun, she thought. Let it be dark of a sudden. So we can talk now, not seeing each other's face.

'Thank you,' Matty said.

'For what? For playing my part in the family dance?'

Our faces hidden. And we will make spells, spin threads, of dreadful things, thin red threads to new lives for you and me. Through the eyes of needles. Through the maze.

'Frank and I . . .'

There's no way out, Matty thought.

'We . . . have a pact. Every night, at midnight, I stand naked in front of a mirror, and say his name. And every midnight, he thinks of me.'

'What, in his cell?' Matty heard a crack in her voice.

'It is a conspiracy.'

Matty scoffed. 'Of masturbation?' She was blushing.

'What else can we do? For now.'

Blushing, because she imagined herself naked before a mirror, running her hand across her stomach, thinking of a man lying on an iron bed beneath a grey blanket. Matty said, 'Oh Cis, I'm afraid for you. I really am.'

'Then be a friend to Frank and me.'

'Of course . . .'

'A real friend. A fellow conspirator.'

They looked directly at each other. Sister talk, thought Cis.

Kiss and tell, kiss and tell, thought Matty.

'All the good love affairs are conspiracies,' Matty said. 'Aren't they?' She paused, then added. 'Rodney is very well.'

'I was going to ask.'

'Yes you were, sister dear.'

'Isn't it difficult, now he's . . .'

'In the Cabinet, a Junior Minister? No, much better. He's got a flat, handy for the Commons. Well, more a little house, south of the river. One of those funny streets, the back of Waterloo station. A secret land, you know? Amongst the winos and the mayhem.'

'Fun.'

'No, not really.' Not really at all. It should be glorious fun. But it wasn't. The fear, walking along the little grey street, most Wednesday afternoons. A glamorous affair, with a Government Minister? Why could she not boast of it, bask in the risk? But no. The worry ate at her.

'Cosy, though?'

'One little sordid thing I do. That's all mine,' she said, looking up with tears in her eyes at the eaves of the house she hated. 'It's all I've got, Cis.'

Don't let her cry! Say something hard. 'And Henry? No horrible mistakes?'

Matty looked at her, sharply. 'You mean stains on clothes? Letters? Bites on my shoulders? No. I keep clean as a whistle.'

But for how long? A thin membrane, a cellophane wrapping, one slit it would take, for the secret to be out and her marriage to be ruined. For Henry would not take it, she knew. He would collapse inside. Implode, the word. Crumple inwardly. A vacuum crushed by atmospheric pressure. She could see what it would to to his face. He would be like one of those dreadful Francis Bacon paintings, eyes and the flesh of his cheeks squashed. And it would just take one simple sentence, 'I sleep with your best friend.' Just one banal mistake, a packet of her lover's cigarettes with the telephone number of a hotel scrawled upon it, fallen from her handbag. Oh the hotels, they did that sometimes, for the excitement, to sharpen the edge of the risk. Or simply to be spotted stepping from a taxi around the back of Waterloo by a mutual acquaintance. She had to police herself all the time and it tired her out. What if this conversation, on a freak gust of wind, drifted up to an open window in the house? She knew she would make a mistake in the end, the one fatal slip, out of exhaustion. Sometimes she wanted to, so she could rest and escape the double life that was slowly wearing her out. Blurt it out, at a dinner party, before Henry's awful friends, and go away that night, walk out of the house, barefoot, a small bag with a few things, and drive three hundred miles to a big hotel by the sea, book in and sleep a whole year, a year and a day . . . But no. Not for me. No great gesture, just this stuck, weary state of things.

Oh well. What does Cis want, she thought. She is after something. She made an effort to concentrate on the grass, the sunlight, and Cecily saying . . .

'Matty. Frank wants to meet him.'

'Yes all right, Daddy will have to meet this thug of yours in the end. I don't know if I want to be there, but I'll help, if I can . . .'

'No. Frank wants to meet Rodney.'

'Our bits on the side? I don't think they'll get on,' Matty said, without thinking. And then stared at Cecily, appalled. What is this? What did she just say?

There was a silence between them. A sudden breeze moved the light material of their dresses, then was still.

'You told this man in gaol that I . . .'

'I told Frank that I know a way of getting in touch with the Junior Army Minister.' Get it all out now, Cecily thought. Don't stop. Hit her with it.

'Cis, how could you? How could you even begin to . . .'

'I never told you what he is in gaol for.'

'I never wanted to ask.'

'Armed robbery.'

A silence.

'Cis, I don't want to hear any more . . .'

But you are, my dear. Hearing it all. Forgive me. Cecily forced her words onto her. 'Frank was sentenced because he was involved in London. But the robbery was in Ireland.'

'Ireland,' Matty repeated, dully. Leaden word for a leaden country, she thought. This is beginning to frighten me.

'Dublin. The Irish Police thought the robbery was for the Provos.'

'The . . .'

'The Provisional I.R.A.'

Really frighten me, numb me. Matty heard herself say, with an oddly light tone, 'And they rob banks?'

'No! It was set up, by British Military Intelligence. Armed robbery, that's why Frank only got seven years. And has spent most of his sentence in an open prison. He kept his mouth shut.'

'Cissy, don't tell me these terrible things, you are draining the life out of me . . .'

'I must tell you!' Cecily shouted into her face.

She pulled back, controlling herself. Must, I must, my darling sister. This is the real world you go on about, that you think you have exclusive rights to, and you're wrong. This is what it's like. It's just beneath our feet, our white shoes, the hems of our white dresses, this smooth grass. This is a touch of it I'm giving you. The underground violence that allows our freedom to stand here, glasses in our hand. This freedom in this English house, our picnics in the sun . . . 'I must. Matty,' she continued, 'when Frank was in Durham gaol, before the open prison, there were Irishmen there. They trusted him. They were good to him.'

'Well, that's . . . something.'

'Frank knows a great deal. He wants to talk to someone.'

'No, no, no Cis . . .

'A great deal. All you have to do . . .'

'No, no . . .'

I'm nearly there, I've nearly done it to her, though I know she'll hate me now. 'All you have to do is say a name to the Junior Army Minister.'

'No.'

'To your lover? In the Government? In your secret

land, round the back of Waterloo station? You told me the number of the house.'

Matty could not reply. She found she was grinding the fist of her right hand into the palm of her left. Was this monster her sister? She looked like her. But it wasn't Cis, mad-cap, free Cecily. Something else was coming out of her mouth. A demon was speaking. 'Are you threatening me?' she was at last able to say. 'A threat, sister?'

Cecily looked over her sister's shoulder into the complex mass of one of the willows. The ragged tapestries of green swung, the light splintering amongst them. The heart of the tree was dark and mysterious. She heard herself say, in a sing-song rhythm, 'People can stand naked in cells. With nothing. Even starve themselves to death. We can give everything away. Strip everything away. And once you do that there's no end to what we can do. Once you don't care about being afraid. Once you go through the gate. Remember the name, Peter Carter.'

There was a pause. Then Matty said, simply, 'What have you done to me?'

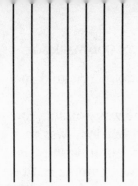

On an autumn morning Cecily sat in her car in the country lane outside the prison. They had planned the moment meticulously. She would wait here, the car parked on the verge, by this gate to a field, around the corner out of sight of the main gate. She had chosen the spot, she had described it to him.

He would walk along the road, between the hedges, towards her, a free man. In her head she had seen it happen so many times.

But it was all wrong.

It's not going to happen. Is it going to happen? Where is he, he's not due yet, he's not here! It's not going to happen.

Stood up at the altar, at the prison gate? Stop this, stop spinning. It's asinine.

She got out of the car and leant against the door. She lit a cigarette. She was wearing a woman's trench coat. She prickled all over, what was she doing, aping Humphrey Bogart?

Fine. He's not coming. Someone else has picked him up while I, a lemon, with french knickers on . . . Why did I buy french knickers? Go over the hedge, into the field, take 'em off. Throw 'em away. Have nothing on under my skirt then, when he walks to the car. What would he think?

When he comes, do I want him to?

When I see him turn that corner, that'll be that. All the promises will have to be kept.

Oh Frank, come on, now my dear. I can't bear this.

She got back into the car and sat at the wheel again. She threw the half-smoked cigarette out of the window. She turned the radio on. A cookery programme on making celery soup. She turned the radio off. She rummaged amongst the tape cassettes in the glove compartment. She stared at one. Beethoven's 'Hammerklavier'. At another. The Eurythmics. Neither made sense. A wasp, lazy with autumnal fatigue, flew in through the car window. 'Damn damn damn!' she said aloud.

There's so much to get right today. If I can't get this right . . .

The wasp buzzed at the rear window. With rage she flipped off her hat, spun round and waved the hat at it. The wasp disappeared. She felt a pain in her left side beneath her ribs. She had strained a muscle. Tears of frustration . . . She thumped the steering wheel with the palms of her hands.

The fag she'd thrown out of the window! Into the grass verge. She hadn't put it out. In a flash of panic, she saw a fire in the hedge. Walls of flame around the car. Her face behind the windscreen, melting like wax. Furious with herself she got out of the car and began kicking about in the grass.

And then she looked up, over the roof of the car. Frank was standing on the other side of the road. He had both his hands in the trouser pockets of a dark suit which was too big for him. He was smiling at her. He had a brown paper parcel under one arm. He actually had a brown paper parcel . . .

He said, 'I feel like the first man on the moon.'

She said, 'You really do.'

He hesitated. 'Do what?'

'Come out with a parcel.'

'Oh yeah,' and he smiled, but the smile died. He looked down. Shy? Oh, he is.

They had planned to lean on the gate to the field. They were going to do all the simple things that had been the stuff of wild dreams in the prison visiting room, the everyday, banal things, like being two lovers, leaning on a gate, looking at a field . . .

But she was frozen. Her throat was clamped and dry. It was the freedom. They could climb over the gate into the field and make love beneath the hedgerow. The freedom terrified her.

Then he walked across, swung round the car and was beside her. Her panic welled. But he stopped . . .

Flinched. It's as bad for him too, she thought. Oh my darling.

'Look I . . .', he began.

'We've got to be at the Registry Office at twelve,' she said. Quick, be quick.. 'Then we'll drive. Straight down to the cottage, like we said? O.K.?'

He looked away. The warmth of a sudden confidence came to her. They were both shy, they were equals.

He laughed. 'I mean I've not got the togs to wear. For a wedding.'

She opened the back door of the car and took out a carrier bag. From it a top hat. The top hat from Moss Bros she had bought the day before. The wedding joke.

She held the hat out. He took it, slowly, as if it were an object of incomprehensible wonder.

Silly, silly, oh please, I hope we can be silly together. 'Let them sneer,' she said.

They moved toward each other. They stopped. He laughed, nervously. They moved again. He put the top hat on the back of his head. 'To the races!' he said. They held their hands out. At the last moment they stopped, inches between their finger tips. They touched hands. He turned her palms over and looked at them.

'Incredible,' he mumbled.

They embraced. His parcel dropped to the grass. They kissed. His mouth tasted of tobacco. They clutched at each other. That tooth stuff, tooth polish. I'll buy him some of that. For smokers. They ran their hands down each other's backs, buttocks, thighs.

'I . . .'

'No.'

'We.' Trying to feel the contours of each other.

'Yes.'

'I . . .' Rucking clothes, in fistfuls. Caressing the surface of her trench coat, as if the gaberdine were her skin. He was clumsy, but soft. Hadn't thought he'd feel soft.

'Yes I . . .' Soft hands.

'It's the . . .'

'I know.' The ricked muscle in her side twinged.

'What's the . . . ?' He looked at her with concern.

'Nothing. There's a wasp.'

'Wasp? What wasp?'

'In the car.'

To her relief, he pulled away from her. He leant into the back seat. He clapped his hands, and, withdrawing from the car, opened them. The wasp was squashed on his palm.

'Frank!'

'Don't worry. Old school trick. One o' the two things I learnt at school.'

'What was the other?'

'Never you mind.'

He flicked what was left of the wasp away with a finger-nail.

She looked into his eyes, as she had done so often in the

prison visiting room. But in the open, under the sky, his eyes seemed a different colour, paler, not so blue and flecked with grey.

'Let's go,' she said. She sensed that he, too, was relieved that they did not have to embrace again. A relief, for now.

They drove away and both of them forgot the brown paper prison parcel which lay in the grass by the gate to the field. It was found the next morning by a milkman driving his float to deliver the morning's milk crates to the prison. He threw away the underwear it contained, but kept the socks and the seven year-old copy of 'Penthouse Pets Of The Year'.

At night, in Kent. Deepest Kent. Deep walls of dark trees, deep night, no city haze of streetlights above, just thick, heavy dark night pressing down upon the little house and its sheltered garden. 'The Cottage'. The family had had it for years, closed up most of the time, lent now and then to friends or friends of friends. There had been childhood times here, crayons and paper on the red tiles before a log fire in the front room, the simple, sparse cottage of a wealthy family, the spartan hidey-hole, smell of burnt logs in the rooms, smell of dank leaves in the garden. In the snug bedroom under the eaves, where an adult had to stoop at the door to enter, Cecily had played games of monsters with a girl of her age from the village. What age? How old was I then? Seven, eight? A windy night, the trees higher than the roof, whipping about, fractured moonlight through the window onto the floral wallpaper of the bedroom. Of wolves, with wings, and witches. It was to this place, holy with family and childhood memories, that Cecily brought her husband of a few hours to make love with him for the first time.

They had married at noon at Kensington Registry Office, with giggles and élan, satirically. They had no witnesses, so they solicited two passers-by, a Rastafarian, who honoured the occasion with a rapping and endlessly incomprehensible poem, and a young mother with a child in a pushchair. They signed the register before a woman official who wore an incongruous blue dress, off-the-shoulder and of ball-gown length. She disapproved of the witnesses. In front of the registrar, after the words were done, Cecily gave the Rastafarian her outmoded Kodak disc camera for a photograph. Oddly, by the rules, they had to mime signing a false register for the photograph, the true record was not for the camera's eye. The paranoia behind this regulation puzzled her. Then to a local pub, for a drink, with the witnesses, the child in the pushchair burbling, happy with packets of crisps bought by Cecily. Then . . . Wedding breakfast! There must be champagne! They dived into a small off-licence and bought six bottles of varying brands and, next door from a street trader, four pounds of oranges. Champagne, and oranges, and air, free air, what more would they need to live? And having kissed the baffled and tipsy strangers who had witnessed their ceremony, they drove out of the London moil of traffic, Cecily praying they would not be breathalysed, drove out, drove down, into the 'Garden of England'.

The cottage. Bolt hole, in the close lanes, a secret territory, in the thick green night, thick green countryside, the Jensens of stockbrokers hidden under hedges, a private landscape where, an hour and a half's drive from London, looking at the moon through a small window, you could still feel alone in the overcrowded world. This darling little refuge, its pokey rooms, the black range in the kitchen, the small staircase with its wooden walls, the old wallpaper of green flowers, was always there in the back of her mind. It waited with its simple chairs, its plain blue cups hung on hooks above the old-fashioned wooden draining board, greying tatty books for holiday reading, Neville Shute and W. H. Hudson. It was always there, unchanged. A woman from the village looked in now and then to see all was to rights, Mrs. Meadows. Oh sod, thought Cecily, Mrs. Meadows. She may drop in, to check all's to rights with the cottage. And find us like this, naked, drunk, playing hide and seek. They hadn't turned the electric lights on. And now all was darkness. Waiting for the moon. They'd used the gas camping lamps though, after night fall. They'd made love by their eerie light on the lawn. Damp, autumn, cold, goose pimples, smeared by grass stains and earth, scratched by twigs and little stones, sleeping bags wrapped around them. Fucking under the stars, under the moon, an end to claustrophobia, in the night shadows of endless recesses, under bushes, under trees. Nebuchadnezzar, the Biblical king, she remembered an old print in an old children's Bible, perhaps it was in the cottage somewhere, in the loft with other old children's books, how it had frightened her. The mad king, eating grass, naked, on all fours, his haunches raised. But now, in the waves of their lovemaking, from dusk into the night, as they struggled through domination and submission to reach a balance between them, to exhaust each other and finally, somewhen, to sleep in each other's arms as equals, as she was determined they would, the image of the degraded king kept coming to her, a condition to be simultaneously feared and desired.

When they had arrived they'd walked into the kitchen. The small, light brown, scrubbed pine table. He stubbed his toe on the lintel of the back door.

She knew at once they must make love. There and

then. If they did not, his clumsiness and her fear would overwhelm them. She knew there was a journey ahead of them, or a dive, deep-sea, a long, underwater swim that they must make, they had to go down together until their lungs almost burst, until they could stand it no longer and at last would swim up to the surface and the air, at night, at one in the sea of their new life. They must nearly drown, now, or there would be no hope for them. She turned to him and begun to fumble with his belt. He brushed her hand away. Get on with it, got to, got to, she thought. She felt closed, cold, awkward, a fury knotting in her. Man, man, 'Man?', come on man . . . She embraced him and kissed him deeply, curling her tongue in his mouth. His arms low around her, grasping the small of her back, he lifted her up, crushing her rib-cage. She pushed him back, to get space between them and began to pull at the buttons on his shirt. Again he brushed her hands away. She glared at him.

'Man? Man?' Her voice was deep, ferocious. A crazed sensation of power flooded through her. She felt as if she were the male, that he was a boy, that she was about to seduce him, to use him in a hard way like a street boy. This insane confidence gripped, this certainty, as if her strength had increased threefold and she could wrestle him to the ground and hold him down and have her way with him.

'Man?' . . .

'I . . .'

'Shut up,' she said and began to pull at her own clothing. And desperately, crudely, he was raising her skirt. She propped her buttocks back on the table's worn edge. Sod, I'll get splinters, but the wood's soft, washed down with so many years of soap 'n' suds, rub-a-dub, God the things you think of at moments like this.

And so they made love for the first time, roughly, painfully for her, for him, she feared, shamefully. She feared she was making him feel he was a ludicrous figure, a cartoon man from a seaside postcard, man with red face and knobbly bum exposed, nonplused before beach bombshell, with his trousers down at his knees. Abruptly he pushed into her, he was livid faced, a man of knots she thought, feeling the tightness in her chest of her own inner fury, this is a knotted man, strangling inside. Her instinct was to push him away, tease him, bring him under control, but she did not for this first time. That was for later, for the long hours of the night ahead. And as the hours rolled, and as their bodies enfolded around each other flowing with the tides and undercurrents of their lovemaking, buffetted then lulled near to exhausted sleep, as they drank champagne then sobered, then as they were silly, showering a whole bottle at each other in the bath, hot water on their legs from the dodgy little water heater, cold spray of the wine in their faces, Cecily screaming with laughter, he not so sure at her wildness, as they grew ravenously hungry and realised they had nothing but oranges and the nearest pub and the village shop cum post office was long closed, the scoured the cottage for something else, anything—and found a tin of ravioli and a jar of olives upon which they feasted deliciously.

And gradually she slowed him, learning how to repel and entice his advances, and then to reverse their roles and for her to be the seducer and he the taken. A 'man's man' you will be no longer, she said to him in her thoughts, running with sweat, pinning him down, making love to him on top, holding his hands together above his head, he all at sea, a woman never gone at you like this before, eh? Man's man? She turned on him, her arse to his face, crossed and held his feet, bent her head towards his ankles and pleasured herself, on and on, shamelessly. I'll wear you out, I'll slow you, 'Man', you'll be raw. We won't be able to tell the taker from the taken. In the morning we'll have each other's face.

Frank crouched naked in the garden, bloody cold, hey Frank, not bad, hey? Hey, oh boy.

In the dark, his and her clothes were strewn about the lawn. They had found sleeping bags in a cupboard in the living room, they were old, Cecily had laughed about being tickled by feathers. Tarred and feathered, the tar their sweet and sticky juices. Where is she?

They had left a Calor gas lamp burning in the little window of the kitchen. He could just see his hand by its eerie blue light.

Brian you should see me now. Your brother's gone moonwalking and he has landed on his feet.

Frank and Cecily had made love on the sleeping bag in the middle of the lawn. Turning on her and being turned, exhausted, beginning to be sore with the bouts of lovemaking, slurred by the drink, a haze of headache at the roof of his skull, he must have fallen asleep. How long?

A few minutes it felt, he'd drifted. And woke, shivering. For a second he saw the cell ceiling, cream paint, a white light in its wire cage. Then the night sky. Where the fuck am I? The marshes? He'd sat up. Goose pimples the size of ping pong balls? And the events of his wedding day hit him, like a magazine of bright photographs flicked through at speed, some of them Cecily, legs up, against floral wallpaper up in the cottage bedroom. Oh dear oh dear. She had scratched him with her nails all the way down his left thigh.

She wasn't there.

Madness, madness, Brian.

I am stark naked. Somewhere in Kent. In the dark. Julius Caesar came this way, saw the Ancient Brits running in the trees, clocking him, their fires on the horizon. He may have ridden over this bit of ground, right here, where this lawn is. Come to conquer a country. Sorry Julius Gaius, I am your great admirer, but come a poor second. I am just here for the cunt.

Talk of her that way. He felt a stab of shame. She was getting to him, he knew.

He scratched at the back of his balls then smelt his fingers. The rich, fishy aroma of the lovemaking filled his nose and the back of his throat.

Madness, madness, my old son.

And pride flashed through him, a fine pride, making the muscles across his chest and upper arms sing. A pride that cut both ways. There was the boast, the pride of manliness, the triumph of the bull who has nothing to prove to anyone, the confidence of a man who had command, saying look at me, getting this away, hey, this is you Frank, bending her over, out of the nick into this, caressing her spine with her bent over the plumpy little cottage sofa, leaning back to get an eyeful of her arse, white skin with a swimsuit mark, the moons of her bum riven with its dark cleft wet with what they were doing, hey hey, madness, mad pride, you are the lad, Frank, you are the one.

And there was the other side of the pride, the half that said, 'What is this? Love?' He couldn't deal with it. The gentleness made him crumple, curl up inside. It was a pride in being so loved and he was helpless before it. The tension, the alertness, the wound-up vigilance of a prisoner was still coiled within him. In his head he was still in gaol. He valued the prisoner's state, the high tuning of the con, and she was threatening it. She made him weak, he could feel it, a sweetness corroding him. Because of this woman, he could let himself down, he could lose sharpness, his skin could go smooth, his arms become puny. He felt she was being moulded into him, down his right side, as if the curves of her woman's body had been grafted into his own flesh. That woman made a woman of him, he'd heard men laugh about that. And yet there was the insane pride in that. A pride that his manliness was being made feminine by her.

Oh Brian, all these years I have missed out on this. You and I, a hundred quid for a girl out of some dump of a club up West, off to some dump of a hotel room, you and I giving her what for, tenners to the doorman, tenners to all, all the way, and you and I having her together giving her a sandwich, the way we used to do that, eh? Brothers in arms, brotherly cockmanship. I tell you all that is nothing compared to this. That wasn't manhood, compared to this.

Frank had told Brian to stay away from his release. He'd not told him of the wedding. Brian was a big problem. In the end Cis would have to meet him. There was no way round that. But people took against Brian.

All come out in the wash. In the froth 'n' suds. Yeah.

Best of all possible worlds, this, thought Frank, pulling the sleeping bag about his shoulders.

'Cis? Where are you?'

She kept still in the dark.

'Sex, champagne 'n' oranges, under the stars,' Frank said. 'You tryin' to murder me or something?' He paused. 'Cis? C'mon.'

She had been watching him against the glow of the gas lamp that was burning in the kitchen window. A silhouette, this magnificent man, crouched, the curve of his back long, hugging a sleeping bag about him. He had fallen asleep, and she had disentangled herself from his arms and legs and the folds of the sleeping bags, taking one with her wrapped about her. She saw him wake and shift. He made little movements with his hand, as if he was arguing with himself. Was he troubled?

She felt the juddering effect of the drink, as she sobered. Had they put a bottle of champagne in the little ornamental pond? Where was the little ornamental pond? She found it, the glass of the bottle wet and cold.

Then, from her hiding place, she said in a whisper, 'Oi Mister, Mister, want an orange, Mister?'

He scanned the dark. She crouched against a pine bush.

'Do I want another orange? Do I, not!' He looked the wrong way. 'Where are y', Cis?'

'Let me play little wifey,' she giggled, scuttling among the bushes, pine needles sharp beneath her feet.

'Little wifey? Please, not done that one yet have we? . . . ' And again he looked for her, the wrong way.

Frank lay back on his sleeping bag, in the centre of the lawn. Cecily looked at him. In the strangely pure light from the lamp his skin was pale, bluey, a long male figure, powerful shoulders, his knees oddly knobbly. Knobbly knees . . . and she giggled again.

'Cis? Stop arsing about . . .'

'To them that seek it shall be given.'

'You what?'

'The Bible.'

'The Bible? After what we been doing, all day and half the night?'

'Prude,' she said. She had already found he was help-less when teased. If the teasing turned to mockery, he would be dangerous. 'Don't you think what we've been doing, all day half the night, is in the Bible?'

'Yeah yeah, Adam 'n' Eve in the stockbroker belt. Fifty quid note for a fig leaf? I'll give it a whirl.'

The moon came out. She walked into the blue light, one hand holding the champagne bottle by its neck, with the other slipping the sleeping bag from her shoulders, dragging it behind her on the grass. He sat up and looked at her. She shifted her weight onto one foot, raising the heel of the other, her knee a little forward. As he looked at her thighs, she felt an ache wash through the muscles in her flanks and her groin. She also felt a rash of goose pimples spreading over her. Then he was shivering too.

'Are you cold?' she said.

'Looking at you like that . . .' He could not finish the sentence. I know my dear, I know, she wanted to say, I know, it's so strong. They were caught in a stillness between them, rooted, looking at each other.

Then he broke it. 'I am a bit parky actually.'

She whirled the sleeping bag above her head. They crouched together, huddling, now shivering uncontrollably, rubbing each other's backs, arms and legs. He opened the champagne bottle. And they were talking, bundled up together, rubbing each other for warmth, the intimate words tumbling from them, easy at last.

'Make your vows to me,' she said.

'I did, Kensington Registry Office, this morning . . .'

'Not their words. Dead words. Real vows.'

'I been making 'em the last five hours. And I tell you . . .' He held up a fist, clenched, 'My blood and my life.'

'We'll have a lot of enemies, Frank.'

'Where I come from, enemies are meat and drink.'

'Where I come from, enemies get in your soul. Violence in the soul.'

He laughed. 'I think I can handle that. Give me violence in the soul any day. It's violence in the back of the head or in the kidneys I was thinking of. Tell you what, you look after the soul, I will look after the muscle. We will be an unbeatable combination.'

'No. The world hates lovers.'

'Jealous, dirty old men, y'mean?'

'Women too.'

'Smell it on us, do they?'

'We shine. It's on our skin.'

'Yeah, we'll dazzle the bastards.'

He doesn't understand, she thought. 'Shining with joy is out of fashion.'

'Never a dedicated man of fashion, myself.'

He's got to understand. 'I saw two lovers in London, in Kensington Palace Gardens. They were very young. They were lying on the grass. He had his hand on her breast. A group of men, drunk, laughed at them and threw a beer can. The girl got up and ran away. The boy stood there, in tears. No, the world hates lovers, Frank.'

He cradled her head, smoothing her hair. 'Hey hey,' he said, close to her ear. 'Unbeatable, that's us.'

'Are we?'

'I am telling you. I am on my vows.'

'Yes.'

His voice was low and hoarse. 'None other.'

'None other.'

'Thick and thin.'

She tried to make light of the words. 'Through oranges and champagne, Frank.'

But that angered him. 'No, I tell you!' He paused.

She turned and put her arms around his neck, looking him straight into the eyes and said, 'In fair and foul.'

'War and peace.'

'Storm and desert.'

Now he began to make light of the intensity of the ritual that had come to them, the gravity they both felt. 'Pissed or sober, my love.'

'Young and old.'

'Through fire and water.'

'Fire and water and blood,' she heard herself say. 'Bloodied and bound.'

They stared on, into each other.

'You're on,' he said.

'I take you on too,' she said.

Suddenly there was a movement in the dark. A sharp sound. Frank started. 'What the fuck's that?'

'Oh no,' said Cecily, 'not the brigadier.'

'The what?'

'The neighbour. A retired brigadier. The bastard's probably got infra-red binoculars or something.'

'I thought we were out in the wilds,' he said, holding her too him, looking about defensively.

'There's nowhere wild in the south of England.'

'No,' he said. 'Look.'

And into the moonlit area of the lawn walked a bird, a wader, its long legs carefully lifted on thin, stem legs, each step deliberate as if thought out and delicately placed, a long curved beak turned one way, then another.

'It's a redshank,' she whispered. 'From the estuary.'

'A visitor,' he whispered back.

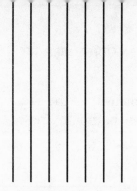

Nothing will be known of the great decisions of state, or of the petty, that were made in our time. Ex-Cabinet Ministers will publish diaries and autobiographies, but they will be self-advertisements, not historical records. There will be no papers that finally come to light to prove that there was or was not a plot by the Secret Services forcing the Labour Prime Minister, Harold Wilson, to sudden resignation from office, there will be no memo revealed from Downing Street to the Ministry of Defence, instructing the British navy to sink the Belgrano in the war against Argentina, no bundle of angry letters bound in tape from one conspiratorial Minister to the other, revealed by a bitter widow to the press twenty years later. For this is the age of the telephone, the late night electronic word into a powerful ear. The real moment of an act of power disappears. The world of political power is, in the electronic age, oral. Careers rise or slide by whispers in plastic earpieces, which even a Minister of State can only suspect, but never prove, took place. Perhaps Harold Wilson was brought down by a plot, but neither we, nor he, will ever know. Perhaps Margaret Thatcher and her advisers did know the Belgrano was steaming away from the Falkland Islands, not towards them, but we will never know they knew. The truth of the historical moment existed for a few seconds on a wire then disappeared with the click of a 'scrambled' telephone receiver, forever. This was the

manner in which arrangements were made about Frank
and his brother Brian. No file in any safe in any office
documented any decision about them. When, later, there
was speculation in the more liberal press and left-wing
magazines, that the British Security Services had
employed South London criminals to act as agents provo-
cateurs in the Irish Republic, playing a dangerous game
of setting Peter against Paul with the Provisional I.R.A.,
it seemed the usual far-fetched paranoia. What? Government officials, conniving at the robbing of the banks of a
foreign country, to gain information about terrorists and
implicate them in criminal activities? It was a story from
the lunatic fringe, along with flying saucers, the discovery
of a second world war plane on the surface of the moon.
Even to the mentality of the security officers and the poli-
ticians who manipulated Frank and Brian, who paid
them for information and sanctioned their escapades in
Ireland, the reality of the scheme was shadowy. There
was a doublethink. It was set up, it was never set up. Telephone calls were made, they were not made. Look at the
telephone wires in the country lanes, squint across the
River Thames at the aerials on the roofs of Government
buildings in Whitehall, pause by a hole opened by telephone engineers in a London pavement to catch sight of
the thick worms of cables that run beneath the streets,
and that is the closest the citizen can come to the wires
and optic fibres that are the corridors of modern power.

Yes, someone has telephoned someone, for sure, Matty
thought. Men on the telephone. How often she had seen
her father, her husband or her lover, through a half-
opened doorway, to catch the odd phrase, 'We'll hold off
. . .', 'He thinks he can do it, you know . . .', 'He doesn't
know that, don't let him . . .' the little shards of business
and politics. Then as she pushed the door and walked

into the room, the click as the telephone is put down, Daddy or Henry or Rodney turning to her. 'Who was that?' He would smile. 'Oh some fool.'

Yes, they've telephoned each other about Frank. That's why I am sitting here. Though really why, why Rodney had agreed at once to meet this awful man her sister had stupidly married, the Junior Army Minister with some hoodlum fresh from gaol, she did not know. 'Anything for a bit of fun,' he'd said. And she knew he was excited, for their lovemaking that afternoon had been more heated than usual. He had hurt her wrists, holding them hard against the headboard of the bed in the small bedroom. Then he'd stood up, pre-emptorily. Could he be nervous?

He is, he's nervous. Now they had been waiting downstairs for nearly an hour and had run out of things to say. Matty could feel Rodney's determination not to look at his watch again. She was glad, because if he did she feared she would scream.

She sat with her legs crossed on the small sofa, in the small house, the 'hidey-hole' in Waterloo. Rodney stood before her, hands in his pockets, legs astride.

The curtains were drawn. The light was a custard yellow from the dowdy shade of a standard lamp. Who had furnished the cupboard-like rooms of their illicit meeting place? They had an anonymity all of their own. Bottles and glasses stood on a dark wood sideboard, far too big for the room. Above it there hung a ghastly print in a gold frame. In a Victorian garden of urns on pedestals, a young man and woman sulked. Autumn leaves were scattered on the paving stones. The print was titled 'Passing Clouds'. Had it been hung there as a joke by whatever Government department was responsible for furnishing the house as a joke? Was there a Whitehall warehouse, full of pale chintzy sofas, plump double beds with wooden headboards, custard yellow lampshades?

Dowdy, yes, she thought. Dowdy mysteries. She liked the musty, hole-in-the-corner house, the windows never open, thick carpets on the little staircase, thick blankets on the bed, thick air, the musty smell of their lovemaking, smells of sleep pervading the house reminding her of an airing cupboard in her childhood that she used to hide in. Matty did nothing at all to the Waterloo house, the 'love nest', no cleaning, no rearranging of furniture, no placing of ornaments upon shelves. Somehow new toilet rolls appeared in the loo and the windows were cleaned. She never saw by whom. And did not care. Here she sought to behave in a full contrariness to how she behaved at home. Here she did not undertake the baking of wholemeal bread, here there was no fussing, no domesticity, no homeliness at all. That was what the affair had to offer for her, a pornography of laziness, of squalor. She wished the house was filthy rather than merely 'dowdy'. But the squalor of Rodney's tastes in bed compensated for that.

Rodney twitched his knee with impatience. Oh come on Cis, where are you? She felt a pain in her stomach. I want to fart. Why not, she thought, with him standing over me. A blarp of a fart. Here I do anything I like. That's the idea. Why not? Pull up my skirt, spread me on the sofa, pull my tights down, blarp! Right in front of him. Let my sister come, with this Frank, this person, and gawp.

But instead she said, 'Why are you wearing a sports jacket?'

'What?'

Tweed. He never wore that. God he's dressing down, to meet Frank. The lower classes. She didn't like this man. His sandy hair, freckled skin, his reedy strength.

But coming here, it's not about 'liking', is it, she said to herself. It's the sinew in him. Sinewy, ruthless, when he made love he often hurt her.

He flicked his wrist and looked at his watch. Scream now?

And the doorbell rang.

'I'll go,' she said, pushing herself up from the sofa.

'Hang on . . .', and he was at a drawer in the sideboard. He took out a hand radio set with a stumpy aerial and said a word into it. What? Echo what?

'My God, what's that thing?' she said.

'Fun, isn't it?'

'I never knew that was there.'

'With the fixtures and fittings.' He put the radio to his ear. 'They're here.'

Watched? She felt the pain in her stomach shift with a twinge of panic. The house watched, what, all the time? 'I'm scared,' she said.

'No,' he smiled. 'This will be amusing.'

'Scared for my sister.'

'Darling, relax,' he said, and kissed her on the cheek, and for a second held her arm hard, almost pinching her. The doorbell rang again and he went out of the room.

Alice in Wonderland, Matty thought, alone for a few moments in the room, Alice getting bigger and bigger at the bottom of the rabbit hole.

A big man, all grey and black, a Bell's whisky bottle in his hand. Black shirt, a grey, lined face, deep lines. Short grey and black hair. Wide shoulders. Black raincoat, open. A stoop of those shoulders? He filled the room. She found herself looking at the belt of his trousers. A black belt, neatly buckled. The whisky bottle glinted, the only colour about him, even his hand was grey, through the black hairs. A presence of silver and charcoal. Oh sister mine . . .

Later, when the intervention of Frank Blake into their lives had worked itself through to its tragic conclusion, Matty pretended, with the bitterness of hindsight, that the first impression he made was overwhelmingly brutal, his sloping shoulders those of a thug, a street brawler. She wiped from her memory that her first reaction was, oh sister mine, what a shy, sweetie of a man you have got your hands on . . .

Very shy. 'Er . . .', he said, staring at her.

Rodney and Cecily pushed past him into the room. They stood there, an edge of hilarity between them in the confined space.

'This . . .', Cecily began.

'Mathilda, yeah?' He held out his hand.

Mathilda? He thinks I'm called Mathilda? 'Matty,' said Matty.

'Oh. Right.'

So awkward! This is just sex isn't it? It's got to be just sex. Cis, you bitch . . . And saw that her sister was radiant with happiness, her skin glossy, her face clear, Cecily at her loveliest, in full definition.

'Glad to meet you,' Frank was saying and she was shaking his hand. His palm was warm, his grip unexpectedly soft.

'Yes. Congratulations,' said Matty taken aback at the aura of success about this man and her sister.

'Oh ta.' Matty saw him blush.

'Accepted,' said Cecily.

'Was it . . .', Matty went on.

'What?' interrupted Cecily, the twang of a single string of sexual rivalry sounding between the sisters.

'Was it good, the ceremony?'

'Well, it wasn't Westminster Abbey,' Frank said.

'No?' And now Matty blushed.

And for a moment they were all stuck in the delicious embarrassment between them. Rodney broke it.

'Right. Drinks?'

Frank raised the bottle of Bell's. 'I got this.'

'Oh, excellent. Please . . .', Rodney said, waving at the sofa. Cecily and Matty sat down, the two men standing before them. Knees again, she thought. Exposure of knees to men. Cis and I have the same legs. Though she's slimmer, always was. I go dumpy, round my middle, I dumple. Sister, cow.

'It's been champagne all the way since I got out. 'Bout time to hit the Scotch.'

'A return to basic values, Frank?'

Matty saw that Rodney's remark bewildered Frank. She came to the rescue. 'Is the cottage all right?'

'As ever,' Cecily said.

'We slept on the lawn,' Frank said.

'Has the weather been that good?'

'We didn't notice,' said Cecily. Riding for a fall, the arrogance of lovers in the first rush of blood, Matty thought. They'll learn.

Rodney handed out drinks. 'We are all on Scotch I take it. As creatures of the world.' He raised his glass. 'To Frank's freedom. To the happy couple. To their honeymoon on a Kentish lawn.'

'Yes, yes!' laughed Cecily and they all drank, only to find the embarrassment had returned.

'Shall we . . .', said Matty. But Rodney was moving decisively, putting his glass down upon the sideboard with a smack.

'Cis, Matty, Frank and I are going out for a while, to talk things over.'

Matty looked at Cis. 'Oh. The men are going outside and may be some time.'

'We'll just amble over the bridge, yes Frank?'

Frank shrugged.

Matty was angry. She felt demeaned. She had imagined . . . she didn't know what. A conspiracy? The four of them, plotting in this secret place, lovers laying plans against the world. She felt hopelessly naïve, sunk in the sofa's cushion below the two men who would now, as men always do, go elsewhere and close the door to rearrange the world. 'Fine. We'll talk amongst ourselves, won't we Cis?'

'Yes we will . . .'

'Girls' talk. You know, the length of men's cocks. That kind of thing.'

'Yes my darling,' said Rodney and leant over the sofa and kissed her on the mouth. She sensed that Frank saw her humiliation. He gestured with a hand.

'Er . . .', he said.

But Rodney was shepherding the big man out of the room. 'Come on Frank.' The front door slammed and the sisters were alone.

Matty forced herself up from the sofa and poured herself another whisky. 'You?' Cecily shook her head.

'Well. I'll give it to you, Cis. He is gorgeous.'

'You think so?'

They looked at each other, then both smirked. Oh what does it matter, what does it matter, sister mine? This little room, floating on the surface of the planet. We know each other so well and here we are.

'Look, Matty . . . Thank you. For making this possible,

Frank meeting Rodney.'

'I don't know. I don't know whether you should thank me.'

'How do you mean?' There was an edge in Cecily's voice. She feels it too, Matty thought. This room, bobbing about, in the sea, but if there's a leak we sink. Are we sinking, even now? Draw back the curtains, see strange fish against the glass . . . 'Matty?'

Matty looked into her drink. 'My lover is . . .' She hesitated. She hated to put fears into words, they became real, it was better not to. But she forced herself on. 'My lover is, well, sometimes a jumpy little man. Like my husband. I must like the type.' She always spoke to Cecily about Rodney this way, she never told her of the steel, the cruelty in him. 'But when I finally got up the courage to ask him to meet Frank . . . And said that name to him, that you wanted me to say . . .'

'Peter Carter,' Cecily said, flatly.

'Sh,' said Matty.

Cecily shot a glance at her. 'What?'

Matty shook her head. Men, microphones, receivers, wires . . .

Cecily's eyes flickered about the room. 'You mean . . .'

'I don't know. I'm frightened, Cis. When I asked him, Rodney just said "Yes. Of course." At once. He seemed to expect it.'

They looked at each other.

'Cis. What do you really know about your brand new husband?'

The look held.

'Nothing.'

'Love with a perfect stranger?'

'Oh yes.'

Matty could no longer bear her sister's gaze. She

turned and went to the curtains. She raised a hand to part them and look out at the night. But she couldn't. An irrational fear of what she would see froze her. Then she felt arms slipped about her waist in an embrace and Cecily nuzzling a cheek into her hair.

'Let's get drunk, big sister,' Cecily said. Matty smelt a sharp scent. It was a man's aftershave, Frank's.

'Ye shall know the truth and the truth shall make you free,' said Rodney. They were walking beneath dark archways on the South Bank of the River Thames, at the back of Waterloo Station.

What the fuck is he talking about, thought Frank.

'The motto of the C.I.A. on the wall of their H.Q. in Virginia,' Rodney continued.

Frank looked down. At the toe of his shoe there stood a plastic cup of coffee, full to the brim, inexplicably abandoned on the pavement's kerb. He looked up. Above, the cliff face of a massive office block, the Shell Centre, leant against the night sky, its stony concrete cold in the powerful lights that illuminated it.

'Spider Man land,' said Frank, his eyes running along the ranks of windows.

'What?'

'Nothing.'

Spider Man, spider net. Don't tie me down, don't come at me, that's when people kill people. I pass, thought Frank. I will not lose my rag.

But what the fuck. Here he was, out in night-time London, with some upper-class face, it was easy, it was walking on water. Long as you don't believe your luck, it'll all come to you, Frank my lad.

As for Rodney, he was acutely aware that this was a damn fool thing to do, which was why he suspected he

79

was enjoying himself so much. 'Acute', to have one's hearing, one's anticipation, tight, to be aware of your weight on the ball of each footstep. He felt the physical intimidation from Frank but he was confident, like a Judo contestant, that he could divert it to his advantage, make his adversary fall headlong at any moment. This is the life, he thought. He felt a rush of excitement. It's true. After all the telephone calls, the words in ears, the subtle interplay of the reputations of powerful men, it is as crude as this.

As the Junior Army Minister, Rodney sat on the Downing Street Anti-Terrorist Committee, as liaison between the political world, in which he was a rising but unseen star, and the world to which his heart, as an ex-Guards Officer, truly belonged, that of Military Intelligence and the uneasy relationship with the other Secret Intelligence Services. Here he was 'in the field', if the concrete bastion of the South Bank arts complex could be described as a field. It was a maverick thing to do, but there was a family connection here. The sister of one's mistress has gone mad. One's mistress is herself embroiled in this business. And it has to be sorted out. Very much sorted out. As a soldier he had never seen action. When the Falklands had blown up he was already years out of the regimental mess and into the softer dangers of the House of Commons tearoom. So when he proposed that he should make the contact with Frank Blake, the committee had pooh-poohed. A maverick gesture. But the Prime Minister had intervened, a love of the maverick there, a puritanical grasp of the sordid possibilities, also an internecine move against the professionals of MI6, the complexity of which he was content not to grasp. The committee had at once agreed, of course, a touch of the electric cattle prod from on high. And here he was.

The only thing was he could not understand a damn thing Frank Blake said. The man's remarks seemed to come out of nowhere. He suspected that, in turn, Frank could not make out anything he said. Piquant, thought Rodney. They don't warn you on those anti-terrorism courses that when you actually make human contact with the criminal mind, you won't be able to understand a blind word that's being said to you.

They climbed up steps that twisted in a maze of grey slabs. 'They built all this for art, you know,' Rodney said. 'Queen Elizabeth Hall? Hayward Art Gallery?'

'Smells of cat piss.'

'Not cat. Human. They're listening to Mozart in there, behind a wall running with the piss of winos. I find that strangely reassuring.'

Now I am not going to get the uncontrollable urge and bop this Charlie one, thought Frank. Am I? I am. Nah, get a grip, think of something else. That cup of coffee on the kerbside. Some drunk. Had a rush of blood to the head. Decided on the spot to dry out. Cup from the stall down under the station, then couldn't face it. Two minutes later, was back on the British sherry. I know the mind . . . and Frank thought of his younger brother, Brian. Exploding man. Don't worry Brian, I'll see you all right, I'll get through this shit, don't worry.

They had climbed up onto Waterloo Bridge to lean on the parapet at the bridge's centre. The river, in full flood, opened London before them. Frank stared at the illuminated dome of St. Paul's, crowded by the dark towers of offices in the City. The dome a woman's breast, Cis asleep, 'the tit o' St. Paul's tickles God's balls', old-time playground song. Old-time. Those blocks round St. Paul's, when did London get to look like that? Like a fucking graveyard. Where they make the money, gravy train, goods yard. I'm not going to say anything to this joker, 'til he says something to me. This is my city. Here I move. Frank realised that, though the man leaning on the parapet with him was younger, he was thin, reedy, slightly hollow chested, a lightweight. He could pick him up by the seat of his trousers and flip him, with one arm, into the water, any time, just like that. This wimp.

'I was warned that you are a knowing bastard,' Rodney said. 'All I am going to do for you is listen.'

Frank felt himself tense, alert. The wimp had steel in his voice. Count to ten Frank, then say it to him, hit him in the face with it. . . .Ten.

'Peter Carter.'

Rodney sighed. 'A common name. Why do you think it is of such importance?'

In the nick, light bulbs everywhere, and straight lines. Everything seen. But unseen, the dark undergrowth, the passing of information, the slipping of dangerous names. Frank could here the Irishman's voice, as if he were there with them on the bridge. 'There's a Brit. Peter Carter.'

Give it another ten. . . .Ten.

'A name that's got you and me together. A real Laurel and Hardy act, eh? The high and the low. Peter Carter is an MI6 officer. Brought in by the S.A.S. to operate undercover in West Belfast.'

Wham, blam, splat. . . .Ten.

'Is he not?'

Rodney was silent. This is simple, Frank thought, a knife through butter.

'Under what is known as the Military Reconnaissance Force. A real bunch of heavies. Specially formed to knock off Micks at Her Majesty's pleasure.'

He paused. Rodney was dead still.

'Really special, that Peter. A loner. In what is known as a Special Duties Team.'

He felt Rodney flinch. Hah! Blood, old man, have I drawn blood?

'Want to know how I know that?' said Frank, airily, feeling . . . I am knocking this geezer all round the park. I know I am. I'm really hurting him. 'A little Irish voice, in the nick. They trust me you see. Well, I was in the nick for robbing banks for 'em.'

'And for us.' Rodney was shocked. What side was this man on? Rodney sensed what he could only describe to himself as depravity, a tangled view of the world from below, that had nothing to do with the world as the Government, or political commentators, or, Rodney assured himself, as ordinary, law-abiding citizens saw it. Did Frank Blake have no sense of good or bad? Probably not. A sensation of moral vertigo disorientated him. This bastard saw himself as a double agent, playing off the Government itself against the I.R.A. The man was a fantasist.

But that's what makes him a valuable commodity. That is why I am here, thought Rodney. We see a way of using him.

'You know,' Rodney said, his voice low, 'you could find yourself in very great difficulty indeed.'

'The spice of life,' said Frank. 'Your Peter, he is marked down. The animals over the water, they know all about him. They really object to a Brit like him being smuggled into their cage. You better get him out of there.'

'You tell me this as a patriotic Englishman, I suppose?' said Rodney, unable to control the sneer in his voice.

'Yeah, I love this country,' said Frank. Adding, to himself, and what the fuck do you know about dear old England, the real, dear old England, you poofy ponce?

A pleasure craft, brightly lit, emerged from beneath the bridge and sailed away from them. A string trio in evening dress were playing. A crowd of well-dressed men and women talking and laughing with wine glasses in their hands could be seen through the boat's glass roof. Cissy's world, that, Frank thought. And this geezer's. Cis. I'll hire a boat like that, my love, when I've got through the shit, when I've got going again. We'll dance down the fucking river, to violins. We will.

'There is no "Peter Carter" on the streets of Belfast.'

Again, Frank felt himself spring alert. There was hatred in Rodney's voice. This guy is a heavy after all, thought Frank.

'There is no such organisation as the Military Reconnaissance Force,' continued Rodney. 'There is no such thing as a Special Duties Team.

'No,' said Frank. 'There in't a place called Ireland either. Nor is there any death.'

And felt his temper go. Snap. A crack on the back of the neck. Scumbag, what is it with these people? What do they think, they can screw the fucking world and no one'll notice? He scoffed. 'You're all playing soldiers over there. Trying out new guns and the fuck knows what. Northern Ireland? It's one big toy shop to you, in't it. You can show off the latest anti-terrorist gear before flogging it to the Arabs. They should put up a football stand along the Falls Road. So all the arms dealers can have a good view.

'That is an analysis,' said Rodney. 'You should work for the Ministry of Defence.'

At the sarcasm Frank saw a flash of light sear across the surface of the river, an electric bolt of anger. Oh Brian I'm sorry. This is what does you in. You lose control. He clenched the muscles in his hands, the tendons in his fingers like claws. Don't move. Go cold, as ice, 'cos this joker is dead. Dead.

'I want ten grand up front. Her Majesty's Government owes me that anyway for the Dublin job. Does it not?'

Violence? Forget it, no one knows the half of it. That little outing in Ireland, the bank, a graze down my leg. What do I remember of it? Caught the car door on my leg. And a smell, paraffin, from the wool over my mouth. Balaclava. A right Robin Hood. I am smelling paraffin, I thought. Could have had my head alight. How did paraffin get in a woolly balaclava? The cashier, little Irish girl, had a face like an egg. Smooth and white, nothing on it at all. Mouth, eyes, nose, wiped away by the fear. Mine much as hers. Then the high after. And everything freaking out. They had us twelve hours later. Brian got away though.

'Ten thousand pounds,' Rodney said. Frank looked at him. Rodney was nodding his head, smiling. The bastard's laughing at me thought Frank.

'Come on! The robbery I went down for was set up by your lot. "Psy-ops" operation. Psychological warfare. Run out of Old Sarum. Sarum, harum, hair-brained scheme. Get some British firm to rob an Irish bank and blame it on the Provisional I.R.A. Real schoolboy stuff. Who dreamt up that little lot? You?'

Hit! A hit! I've hit it! Not smiling any more, mister? No you are not.

'Some git like you? A bright idea. Back-fired did it? What happened? Wouldn't the Irish Special Branch play ball? The Micks get uppity did they? Didn't take to all these Oxbridge chaps coming over, letting East End lager louts like yours truly loose on the Emerald Isle, in the banks of Old Ireland? Runs deep, don't it, this funny old world.' He paused. Yeah, he thought, the world running.

The river down there, blood in my ears. Run, run.

They stared at the water for what seemed a very long time. Then Rodney said, 'Mr. Blake. You are less than the shit on the boot of the youngest soldier putting his life on the line over there.'

'Don't worry. I know that,' said Frank, a sense of calm flooding over him, feeling his shoulders and arms loosen. I am equal to this bastard and here we are, on this bridge. 'I am not bitter. I am loyal. I know my patriotic duty.'

'Do you indeed.'

'I tell you in good faith. You've got a man over there, his name is Peter Carter, and he will be very dead if you do not pull him out, now. There.'

'And you have more information, to sell.'

'That I know about this Peter, shows you don't it? C'mon, don't piss me about.' Frank laughed. This was glorious. 'That I even know the name, put you out here with me. On Waterloo Bridge. Don't get me wrong. I want to do my bit. For a price. I am an entrepreneur. Which is all the rage these days.'

'What you are', said Rodney, angrily, 'is a cowboy and a fucking liability.'

'That is me,' said Frank, with a shrug. 'South London's answer to John Wayne. But tell me, one patriot to another . . . All these schemes, using villains like me, the cloak and dagger crap, the whole caboodle. What's it for?'

And Rodney had a sudden insight that shocked him. My God, he thought, just a twist, a slight rearrangement of the times we live in, and this bastard could be my colour sergeant. I could be acknowledging his salute upon a battlefield then shaking his hand.

'I mean,' Frank continued, 'what do you hope to achieve?'

'Victory,' said Rodney. 'Victory.'

'Yeah,' said Frank, suddenly weary. 'To me it's just a mouthful o' woolly paraffin.'

'What?'

'Never mind.'

Rodney took out an envelope from an inside pocket. Frank could not, at first, catch what was being said to him. It was so simple, it was all coming to him, easy as that.

'An account in the name of Frederick Wallace has been opened at the National Westminster Bank, the Lambeth North Branch, Westminster Bridge Road. It is, at the moment, empty. If what you say has any . . . worth, there will be a deposit. Here is a cheque book and cheque card, made out to that name at that branch.'

He held out the envelope. Frank stared at it. Like an old-time bookie's runner, this. Or being slipped hard porn in a brown paper bag.

'Taking a risk aren't you?' said Frank.

'I am a sporting man,' Rodney said.

'The gee-gees?'

'River trout. Ever caught a brown trout?'

'Fuck off,' said Frank.

'Don't try and bounce a cheque, will you Frank? The man who is your real bank manager could at any moment withdraw the account. Along with half of your skull.'

'I want cash.'

'Don't be silly.'

'Yeah.' And Frank saw it. The money would be dirty. Stolen, numbers known. so they could lift him, anytime. Don't be fooled. When these people give you something, they are taking away from you. Always. Taking your life. And all your luck? Nowhere.

'You know your trouble?' said Frank.

'I have no idea I have any trouble.'

'Yeah you do. You're a hard bastard, deep down. Under all that.'

'All what?' said Rodney.

Frank ignored him. 'But you think it's goodies 'n' baddies over there, don't you. We Brits the goodies, the Micks with the guns, baddies. But it's not. When you get up close, when you get mixed up in it . . . it's nothing to do with goodies and baddies at all.'

'Really?' Rodney found all this intolerable. 'What is it to do with, then?'

'Oh you know,' said Frank, grinning. 'Death. That's the side we're all on, in't it? Death. May I?'

And Frank took the envelope, pocketing it quickly. 'Here's to victory,' he said.

'Unsexed.'

'What?'

'What I am,' and Matty giggled. She and Cecily were now well and truly drunk. Matty looked at the lamp standard in the little room. A glow, like an American space rocket on TV, was developing beneath it. It was about to take off into the ceiling. Out of the roof of the house. A lamp standard seen, a trail of sparks, ascending over night-time London? Whoops. She felt her stomach swing. A muslin bag on a string full of whey. Cheese making, which she did, in the country. She shook the image away.

'We are, unsexed. Sitting here. Our knees are getting big.'

'Matty . . .'

'We are parked. To go blubbery. Blow up, like big balloons. Have we got drunk?'

'We have.'

Matty's tongue seemed huge and heavy, pounds of weight, but when she pressed it to her teeth they seemed

tiny, delicate and far away. 'I've got the "big-little",
badly,' she said.

The 'big-little' effect. It was something they talked of
and shared in childhood, an overwhelming sense they
would have at night, just before they went to sleep, of
being both massive and delicate. Weight and proportion
all askew, head and chest vast boulders, feet at the bottom of the bed miles away and minuscule, ankles so thin
and brittle they could never support you . . . When this
flickering hallucination returned in adulthood, as it did
occasionally, to Matty it seemed to be a warning, a vision
of the deformed world in which it was impossible to
move.

'Shall I try to make some coffee?' said Cecily.

'No, I'm all right.' Matty poked out her tongue. The
lamp standard returned to the floor. The nausea steadied.
She grimaced. 'It's just you and me. And them. We're all
. . . Not old. It's just us. So why all this?'

'Why all what?'

Oh you catch so much, in a spiral, you see it all, swirled
together, all of us, all of 'it' . . .

'This. We in this room. Our fellahs out there. What's
chopping . . . Divide, dividing us up?'

'I . . . think I will make that coffee.'

Cecily stood. Matty panicked. Oh Cis, I can see it, I
know what is being done to us, I can touch it. With my
tongue. I . . . She wanted to say that they were young,
still, that, that the four of them could do anything they
wanted, that, that there was only this game that they
were caught in, game of being who they were, she the
adulterous wife, you, Cis, the bride of a criminal, Rodney,
an officer of state, that really they were free, there was no
reason why they should not stop all this, now, that, that
they should love each other now, go off to a restaurant,

hand in hand, that, that hand in hand they could run along the embankment, leap up and fly off, over the river tonight, that, that there was only fear, while if they held hands they wouldn't fall . . . But she could not express what she felt, the alcohol tangled it up and it surfaced only in trite phrases that dismayed her. And then Frank and Rodney were back, and coming into the room.

They were grinning, rubbing their hands, their faces were flushed. So it was cold, cold outside . . .

'Gossiped amongst yourselves, girls?'

'Yes,' said Matty. 'Girls' talk. The length of men's cocks compared.' Did she slur? 'And what did you talk about? F-football?'

'Yes actually. Frank here is a Crystal Palace supporter.'

'For my sins,' said Frank.

Cecily was laughing. 'They have. They really have talked about football.'

'I think we've got some catching up to do on you girls,' said Rodney. 'Let's get smashed.'

'Your sister was well gone,' said Frank.

The first pillow talk, thought Cecily. They had gone from Waterloo, after a few drinks, the occasion stiff and awkward, back to her Kensington flat for the first time. Now they lay in each other's arms, smoking, the duvet thrown upon the floor ('I can't stand these fucking things,' Frank had said), the bedsheet and their skin pale in the streetlights that slatted through the Venetian blinds. The blinds were a relic of her days in the office. But now no more 'Young Businesswoman of the Year' pretence, no more metal Venetian blinds and smart black leather shoes. From now on, floppy boots and thick curtains . . .

Oh she was tired. The three days and nights of tumultuous lovemaking in the cottage had left the muscles of her arms and thighs liquid and weak. Her skin sang. Her nipples were intolerably sensitised, her labia were sore. Then she had realised with a flash of vindictive pride that he was as sore as she, and though he had resisted (you stupid hulk, stupid brute, still shy at odd moments after all we've done), she had carefully smeared him and her with Savlon cream before they folded tenderly into each other, to make love simply and fully. She felt him touch the end of her womb.

Then, as they lit their cigarettes, she thought, 'Oh, where are we going to live? Too small here. He is so . . . big.' And as the tide of sweet exhaustion rippled over her, she realised that all those months and years while Frank was in prison, what had now become an unreal past, she had thought of only these first days and nothing of what might lie beyond them. But what the hell, what the hell, why care?

I've done it, I've stripped myself of the old ways. The plans are made. I am with him. Everything has changed. I told Matty I do not care, nor do I. Actually . . . Daddy will give us the cottage. If Matty and her fool husband scream, let them. She stretched a leg, she extended the toes of a foot, luxuriating. Fuck Matty and Henry.

'But did you like her?' she said.

'She's great,' said Frank, falsely, she thought. We're going to have to find a way to talk like this . . .

'What did you think of her fellah?'

There was a silence.

'A bit, er, officer material there.'

'Very much so.' She paused. 'Did you get on with him?'

'Like a house on fire. His house not mine, I hope.' He paused. 'Look, er, your sister and him.' And again he was silent.

You've got to do this Frank, I'm going to make you, you've got to talk.

'You know it's very secret, that, between them. You must never breathe a word, when you meet Daddy.'

'Meet him?'

'Don't jump. Of course you must meet Daddy.'

'You better meet Brian, and all.'

A silence.

'Meet who?'

A name, suddenly this name from him. And he was defensive, she could feel his caution.

'My brother, Brian.'

'You never told me you've got a brother.'

'Didn't I?'

No you did not. Be careful, she said to herself, this is the first catch. The first hiccup. Why? What's wrong with this brother?

Cecily knew that Frank's mother and father were dead, the father in the late sixties, a docker his lungs ruined by unloading asbestos, when there were still docks in London. They had moved from the East End to Peckham in South London. 'Mum thought the air was better.' After his father's death they had been offered compensation. Frank had told her of it, angrily. A scale for 'pain and suffering', maximum amount ten thousand. You got points out of ten for pain and suffering. Frank told them to stuff it. He had all the East End pride of looking after his own. After his father's death, his mother had hung on. Cecily had gained a visual impression of her, a small woman, sparrow-like and light, sitting quietly in an armchair, in the flat in East Dulwich that Frank had bought for her. The impression took a knock when he showed her a photograph of a huge woman with massive arms folded and a wide grin above an ample double chin. It was signed, in big letters of blue Biro, 'Love, Mum.'

But brother?

So much a mystery to me, my husband. 'All right then,' she said.

'All right what?'

Don't be obtuse Frank. Don't be like this. 'All right let's meet Brian.'

'Yeah well, You will, sooner or later.'

'Frank, what's the matter?' What was she sensing from him? Was it a kind of . . . sorrow? She could feel him softening. He put his arm about her. Yes, it's sorrow. Love fired through her. I love this man to the ends of the earth. She closed her eyes to mask the uncontrollable tears.

'It's just that . . . I've not got round to family,' he said, softly. 'Where I come from, family runs deep.'

'Where I come from too,' she said, a choke in her voice, desperate not to let him see she was crying for he would think she was miserable, when she was not at all.

But he said nothing, just held her quietly, then stroked the back of his hand across her eyes.

She calmed herself to say, 'What were you going to say, about Matty and Rodney?'

'Yeah. She's family now.' And again fell silent.

Now he was beginning to infuriate her. Oh the swings and roundabouts. 'Go on! Tell me what you mean.'

'She should be careful with that one.'

'How do you mean? Frank! Frank!' She sprung round on him, straddled him, and pounded on his chest.

'Hey! Hey!'

'You great big hulk. What, what are you trying to say!'

'Nah, leave off!'

She gripped him by his ears pushing his head against

the pillow. 'What? What?' Then leant down and sank a deep kiss into his mouth and then relaxed, smoothing a hand across his chest, sliding a knee along his inner thigh, simpering to send him up. 'What, mister, what are you on about?'

'All right, all right!' he laughed. 'It's just . . . When I went for a leak, after we'd got back. Went upstairs. And I had a sniff round the bedroom.'

'You . . . went into their bedroom?'

'Yeah, y'know, old habits die hard.'

'Do they.'

'Anyway, they got these ropes. On the bed.'

'Ropes?'

'Tied on the end of the bed, and lying there, across it. Ropes of . . . sort of pink silk.'

Oh Matty, no.

'Funny old world, in't it.'

She felt numbed. 'God, Frank. You think someone is close to you. Your sister. And all the time you have no idea. What they're going through, what they're suffering.'

'I have that with Brian.'

Brian, Brian, what is this brother, a helpless innocent, a saint he has a mission to shelter? She felt that, for Frank, even the name of his brother was something gentle and vulnerable, she heard how he cradled his name with a softness in his voice.

'Just tell your Matty to be careful,' continued Frank. 'He is the genuine article, that one.'

'How do you mean?'

She raised herself on the bed. He was staring across the room, his face blank.

'Are you going to tell me? What Rodney had to say to you?' she said, evenly, as if it did not matter at all. Later she was to remember this moment, when she knew that

94

she would always be excluded from the secret of what her husband really was. She recalled that in his silence there hung, as if from a hook in the ceiling, the nebulous, ill-defined shape of what their future together was going to be, a glutinous crystal ball, bluey and clouded, shot through with darkness.

'Well?'

After what seemed a long, long time, he spoke. 'You will know the truth and the truth will make you free. That's what he said.' He laughed. 'But don't worry. I can handle it,' and he turned upon her, to take her in his arms.

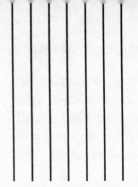

Don't worry, leave it to me, life is a doddle, we are ahead we are winning, these are the days of triumph, laurel wreaths, bread and circuses. These are the days of miracle and wonder, don't worry about a thing, no don't you worry, my love.

Nor did she. And nine months after she married, Cecily found herself lying on a beach on the island of Crete. There was sand, there was sea, there was light.

Fine, she thought.

For she had discovered at once that the best way of living with Frank, his family and the curious hangers-on who appeared then disappeared like passing players in a medieval court was once every week or so to look up to see where you were and not panic, but just say, 'Oh. This is where I am. Fine.'

The notion that she could mould him, bend him to her will, that she could change this difficult, wayward, loving man, evaporated. A laziness floated her away on the weeks of life with Frank, the confusion, the changed plans, the sudden enthusiasms, the restlessness.

These were months of silky pleasure for Cecily. She went with the rippling, chaotic stream of Frank's life, his unfathomable meetings and movements about Britain and the continent. It was a game, she had her eyes shut as long as she could bear, for weeks, then she would open them to ask, 'Where am I?'

Fine. I am in a pub at Shepherd's Bush. Best pub in

London for an early evening drink, fine. It's horrible. Frank had disappeard upstairs with two Irishmen, who came up to us. He pretended it was a chance encounter, but I think they were expecting us. Or expecting him. An hour ago. He is coming back, through the bar, without the two men. Sorry about that, doll. Let's go up West, the night is young. Fine.

And fine. I am in the Gleneagles Hotel, a helicopter is coming down past the window to land on the lawn in front of the entrance. 'Let's spend a fortune,' Frank had said. 'Let's lash out like crazy.' Fine. And now he is saying, 'I've got the screaming heebies. The fucking place is full of Yanks. Sorry love, let's go home.'

'These are the days of miracle and wonder.' The trick was to stay in bed all morning, always, to get your sleep.

She knew that, in the end, perhaps, but not yet, she would have to ask herself what is this dissipation? What am I becoming, a gangster's moll?

And where am I now, this isn't 'home', the cottage, the Kent woodland, this is the Berlin wall. I am out shopping, in Berlin, Frank is doing business for the afternoon and I am looking at the wall. They had been in a bar, a quiet, old-fashioned, wooden-walled German bar. A man had come in. He said nothing, but was he one of the men I saw in the pub, at Shepherd's Bush, a month, no six weeks, ago? Anyway, I am looking at the Berlin wall. Fine. it is painted with graffiti, from spray cans, like the New York subway. Am I really in New York? With a screech of metal, would the Berlin Wall begin to rattle and slide away . . . ?

Often when she 'opened her eyes' and 'looked up', it was night. She would see a round table, a heavy linen tablecloth of deep pink spread upon it and upon the table-cloth champagne and plates of seafood. The men guzzled the food, while the women around the table, and there were always women, younger than herself, left the lobster, the clams, the oysters barely picked at. Beyond the table, there was a floorshow. The floorshow gave some indication of the country you were in. Castanets, your Spain, veils, your Morocco, leather, your Germany, a striptease, your England.

Cecily enjoyed the evenings in clubs. They were oddly grave and formal. It was like a court, she and Frank sat there, a king and a queen, conscious of being looked at, observing unspoken rules of dignity. There would always be other royalty present, at the best tables, with whom it was important to make diplomatic contact before the evening's floorshow and drinking could get under way. The men spent a great deal of time standing up, to greet other men who came over to make themselves known, to be acknowledged and to acknowledge, to make sure the complex scene was in balance and harmony. She imagined all of them painted in a vast mural, as some crass allegory, 'Life—The Passing Show . . .', and there she would be at the corner of the canvas, an unknown woman in the odd clothes of the period, her shoulders bare, stared at in a gallery hundreds of years from now.

'Right. Crete.'

'Where?'

'We've got this villa. In Crete. Long as we want.'

'Villa?'

They were eating bacon and eggs in her Kensington flat. They had just come back from Swansea. Why had they gone to Swansea? They had spent the evening in a packed pub listening to a Welsh country-and-western band. The barmaids were dressed not as cowgirls but as English milkmaids, in bonnets and off-the-shoulder frilly frocks. No doubt Frank, as usual, had had 'to see a man', but she had not seen him see a man. She enjoyed the evening hugely. They came back by train, first class, early that morning. And tomorrow, Crete? Cecily found the incomprehensible travelling, the zig-zagging about, was becoming normal to her. When will this pall, she thought. When will I weary of this?

'What villa?'

'This Greek villa. That this Greek has lent us. Time for summer hols.'

'What Greek?'

'A Greek Greek,' smiled Frank, with a shrug.

Cold marble floors, shutters, big soft white armchairs which slid over the floor. The villa was on the outskirts of the Cretan resort of Aghios Nikolaos, a pretty town, with a little bridge over a lagoon, its prettiness fussed away by tourism, the streets crowded by holiday-makers shuffling along the narrow pavements overhung with tat, funny sunhats, blow-up plastic Greek dolls, leather bags.

The villa seemed anonymous, unused, the large cool rooms were white-walled and sparsely furnished. It had just been built, perhaps no one had yet lived in it at all. A cement mixer stood by a side wall, as if builders had not yet collected it. 'Great, this is great!' they had shouted when they arrived, opening their suitcases, pulling out their clothes on the floors, running from room to room, opening and slamming doors.

And they had gone out at once, to this beach.

'They', that is Cecily, Frank, Frank's brother Brian and his girlfriend, Elsa, a foreign girl, perhaps a Dane, or a Swede, Cecily was uncertain. Elsa did not bother to enlighten her. Now, on the beach, topless, her slight body lightly suntanned, the bottom half of her bikini a black G-string, Elsa seemed self-contained and indifferent. This beautiful young woman was with Brian and that was that. Cecily did not understand it, because Brian . . .

Brian, oh God, Brian. She had steeled herself to meet Frank's legendary brother. But the shock had still been prodigious. She knew she was safe with him, because she was now 'family'. But he was so big. Short, but so very, very big.

But there is sand there is sea there is light.

The sand, in the small bay of the resort, was spread there by the town council, so the beach was artificial, and smoothed every morning and evening with long wooden rakes by the seemingly endless supply of local lean young men, who in-between the ritual beach cleansing spent the day hiring out windsurfing boards and wrestling with each other or playing on children's swings at the back of the beach. The sea, turquoise, pale and clear, shone near its edge with the rainbow iridescence of suntan oil washed from the bodies of bathers. Further out there was a diving raft. The light made the figures upon the raft waver, become stick-like, their arms narrowing to points. She put on her sunglasses. The light darkened, the swimmers upon the raft became silhouettes, the islands of the complex coastline about the resort, their doodled sky-line jagged in the haze, seemed ugly. Crete seemed ugly.

Driving in their hired car from Heraklion airport along the north coast, the island of Thera was a black stump two miles out to sea. Said by the locals, and the guide books, to be the site of the legendary Atlantis, was that pile of ash dumped in the sea the country of science-fiction dreams, a lost golden age? Along the coast the breeze-block hotels, 'Aphrodite', 'Sandy Cove', 'Zeus', were stuck up in the treeless landscape above tiny beaches cornered amongst rocks. Holiday slums. So this is paradise, she thought, it's a slum.

I must stop this, she said to herself, shifting on her

beach towel. It is lovely here. The light is brilliant. It's a brilliantly lit slum. She took off her sunglasses.

I hate it. No I love it. Hate it. Oh what the hell, I'll love it here.

She turned over on her towel and looked sideways. There was an olive tree, marooned on the beach. In its branches, tied by a long lead that let it scamper about the tree, was a monkey. Its tight, tiny face stared at her.

'Sunny Greece!' said Frank. 'Get the olive oil on your bums, here we go, here we go . . .'

'I want some brandy. What do the wops here call brandy?' said Brian, thick legs braced apart to stop himself swaying, his bulging belly hanging out over minimal swimming trunks.

'Metaxa,' said Frank.

'Always the fuckin' scholar, in't he.'

Here come the Brits, thought Cecily, aware of the shock-waves they were spreading along the beach.

'Lovely here, eh doll?' Frank said to her. 'The sand, the sea, who needs damp grass on an English lawn eh, my love?'

Cecily looked at the monkey in the olive tree, who was now slowly scratching his genitals.

'Tell you what Elsa, wiggle your bum over to the bar. Get us a bottle o' brandy,' said Brian.

'Sorry,' said Elsa, in the broken English Cecily wondered whether she was affecting for self-protection. 'You are wanting what?'

'Yeah!' warmed Brian to his theme. 'Not a bottle, get a jug. Fuckin' jug with fruit floatin' about.'

'That is sangria, that is Spain.'

'All wopland in't it? All the fuckin' same.'

A man without any redeeming qualities whatsoever. He must work on it, thought Cecily. Does he shut himself up alone and practise being so utterly repellent? Vomit in front of the mirror, to get it right? For Brian was often sick in public.

'No, brother, it is not. The stuff in the jug is Spain. This is Greece, here it is retsina and metaxa.'

'You what?'

Frank threw himself onto his knees, close to Cecily. He shook his head, mockingly. 'Get my brother, Cis?' He often adopted this tone, talking to her before Brian. 'All the dreams of improving the working man, all your "O" level languages, your Odes of Horace, your Oliver Cromwell, your mass literacy . . . has put upon a beach in Greece, Brian's body. Modern democratic man.'

Brian swayed, puzzled. 'I've put a lot of work into this body,' he said.

'Yeah,' laughed Frank, scrambling to his feet, throwing handfuls of sand at his brother, who just . . . swayed. 'Yeah! Oil tankers o' booze, centuries of the working man's aspirations . . . Days and nights of abandon on two legs, in't you brother?'

'You what?'

'You are wanting?' said Elsa.

'Anything to drink, sweetheart, just anything,' said Frank, giving her behind a slap. She laughed, touching his chest with the nail of a finger, then ran off along the beach. Frank turned and caught Cecily's eye. He blew her a kiss and smiled.

'I'm going to swim. Out to that raft,' announced Brian.

'Storms in the Med! Coming?' Frank held his hand to her.

'Where's me snorkel?'

'Give him his snorkel,' said Frank.

Cecily reached for her beach bag and Brian's snorkel,

the best that money could buy, with heavy vizor and a nose clip.

'Thanks Mum,' said Brian.

Oh God.

Here I come, deep-sea diver!' shouted Brian, and he lurched with a stumbling run into the sea to crash into a belly flop and, with surprising energy and spray, began to swim, head down, out to the raft.

'What a lunatic, eh?' said Frank.

'Your brother and his whore,' said Cecily, trying to sound neutral, trying to sound nothing at all.

'Elsa? She's from Amsterdam.' He paused, looking down at her, dark against the sheen of light from the sea. 'Everything all right?'

'Hunky-dory.'

'Bed, we'll get a sunbed for you . . .'

'Everything is wonderful.' Of miracle and wonder.

'We said it would be a laugh here, it is and all, eh? The town's a bit touristy, bit rough, but you need that now and then.'

'Oh I like a bit of the rough.' I don't mind this, I don't mind it at all, so why am I bitching, why am I carping? Don't worry about me, Frank.

'Look, when we get back, to London, we'll move into the Savoy.'

'Frank, this is our first day here, don't let's . . .'

'No no it's all right, Cis. Back in London we'll move into the Savoy. Fucking suite. View o' the Thames. The lot. The rough 'n' then the smooth. Freshen the jaded palate and all that.'

'Trinculo's feast?'

'Yeah decadence, why not?' He laughed. 'Load's o' offal, a spew up in the old vomitry, then just . . . one . . .

sweet . . . almond. The Romans knew it all. Roman style, that's the life, 'long as your liver lasts.' He lowered his voice. 'Is it Brian?'

She said nothing, thinking, oh Frank, I'm in free-fall. Where were you most of last month? While I kicked my heels down at the cottage? Before you reappeared, then we were off to Swansea, were we in Swansea? Why? No. I can't, I won't, I don't want to ask what the hell you're up to. I will not because I because I sort of know.

And, as if she had spoken anyway, he said, 'You know what I'm up to.'

'Do I?' She crossed her arm across her eyes, thinking, oh yes, I heard about you on the news at the cottage. Transistor radio. A sub post office in Dundalk? That's my Frank I thought, peeling sprouts. Cold water, little knife in my fingers.

'Cis . . .'

'I'm in free-fall, Frank,' she managed to say, flopping her arm away from her face, her eyes closed.

She felt him tense. She was worrying him. A pull on the strands between them, the nerve roots that linked their skins and tied them, that had grown like tendrils into one another, nurtured by the intensity of their lovemaking. Like Gulliver, she often thought, tied down by tiny Lilliputian ropes. They were bound, nervous system to nervous system, millions of little roots, they were becoming, emotionally, like Siamese twins. Of course she knew what he was 'up to'. How could she not?

I've touched him, she thought. He's hurt, now he'll fool about, to get out of it.

'Yeah, free-fall,' said Frank and stood, fooling about. 'It's called flying. Try it. Look, like in the dreams. I had 'em all the time inside. You put one foot in front of the other and . . .' He walked in the sand, arms spread wide as if on a tightrope. 'Dead simple.'

'Let me come with you.'

'Fly.'

'Let me come with you. The next time.'

He dropped his arms to his side, he lowered his head, looking at the sand at his feet.

'The next time you do what you do. The next raid. Take me.' He was dead still, now she was almost hissing at him, shocked that she was saying this, feeling each syllable go wrong, totally misjudged. 'Frank? A woman can wear a stocking over her head. Women carry arms for the Provos. Why not?'

He was silent and dead still, looking down.

I have offended, I have trespassed, she thought, I have desecrated the sanctuary. A nausea stirred in her. He thinks he is a man who walks in the desert and talks with God in holy places. He thinks that to take a woman would defile him. This is impossible between us, it was always going to be.

Frank looked up and was speaking, as if she had said nothing. 'Yeah. Brian is a scumbag. But it's family. It runs deep. And he's got a big heart.' And again he was playing, fooling, raising his arms, kicking sand. 'And! We are in our great good fortune, eh? Fucking Greece? Adventure, my love! Right?' He stopped kicking the sand and stared at her. 'Right?'

Nothing behind his eyes. Closed. The door to the inner sanctum, slammed shut. He is a criminal. So she touched her beach bag and said, 'Do you want your snorkel too?'

'All the gear, eh? For an 'oliday? All we need now is, relax. I mean, c'mon Cis, we are up and away.'

'Yes,' she said. And smiled. She saw him flood with relief.

'Brian's idea, snorkels. Big kid he is really. Yeah, give me mine, I'm going for a swim, look at the fishes in the sea.'

She handed him the snorkel, the ridiculous thing. He bent over her. She went cold. He hesitated, then kissed her shoulder.

'It's all great, Cis,' he said. 'You know you love it,' and he ran into the sea, athletic, diving, his legs together and straight, a clean line, hard calves covered with hair, then disappeared beneath for an alarmingly long count to surface further out and swim with a leisurely crawl towards the raft. A beautiful swimmer, concentrated and compact, a beautiful man, so secretive and closed up, she thought, watching him leave the shore.

'Yes I do. I do love it,' she found herself saying, out loud.

She closed her eyes. The monkey tethered to the tree chattered. A way off, the Greek boys argued and talked incomprehensibly, though she knew they were boasting to one another. Prowess, feats, youth, sex, arrogance, in the debased language of the ancient Gods. Who were, anyway, also boastful, arrogant, murderous, she thought, all preening themselves. Not hairy though, in the sculptures. Did Hermes and the boys shave their legs and chests? Body-shaved males, with dangerous powers, all murderers . . .

'You want to drink?'

She opened her eyes. The all but naked Elsa stood before her, in each hand a bottle of metaxa brandy.

'No,' said Cis.

'I do not, it destroys too much.'

'Yes?'

Elsa looked out to sea and laughed. 'Oh! They are on the raft! Brian is belly-flopped!'

'Indeed?' said Cecily.

'You come now, into the sea?'

Cecily shook her head. Elsa hesitated, with a shrug, not knowing what to do with the bottles of brandy. Then she put them in the sand beside Cecily's beach bag and walked down the slope of the beach to the water, which she tested with a toe then waded in, aware, Cecily saw from the studied nonchalance of her movements, hands raised to her hair lifting her breasts, of the criss-cross of invisible lasers from men's eyes that bored into her body. Cecily sighed and closed her eyes.

Behind her eyes, the curved pink dome, bursts of green from the retained bright images of the beach, the sea and the sun, began to turn then spin as she neared sleep. Dream images rose and neared, Brian, squat, floated towards her over the water at uncanny speed, grinning, he opened the door of an old-fashioned safe in his belly, inside the monkey scratched his balls. Then the sea again, and, with a whoosh of water, Elsa soared up naked and dark against the sun, she spun in mid-air, dipped and was flying at Cecily. She had the monkey's face. About to bite. With a jolt Cecily woke.

Trash dreams.

She looked about the beach. It was in the midday sun and heat, bluey to her eyes. Hell, she'd get burnt. Frank, Brian and Elsa were nowhere to be seen. Was that them, on the raft? She couldn't make out. The beach had emptied, umbrellas had been folded upon their poles. The mad and English pink, out in the worst sun of the day. She'd forgotten about Mediterranean holidays, the assault course, under the sun's ultra-violent hammer. There was a dry rind on her inner lip.

She turned over. At the back of the beach there was a figure. A man. In a black suit. Was he wearing a black suit, in the heat of high August? He had a stick.

Was she alone with him on the beach? Her eyes, still

tired by the sun, saw everything as blue, tinged with violet, bleached out like a faded colour snapshot. She looked at the olive tree. Even the monkey had gone, leaving her alone with the black figure, which seemed to waver and lean upon its stick. He was walking towards her.

She turned on to her back, to ignore him. And waited. She heard the scuff of sand. She tilted her head back, and saw, upside down against the cloudless sky, the man with the stick looming above her. A drawn head, bony, a man of forty, boyish but thin.

'Mrs. Wallace?' he said. English. Educated.

She lay there, dead still, her head tilted back.

'Mrs. Frederick Wallace? Or should I say, Mrs. Frank Blake? Cecily?'

Dead still, staring.

'But what is in a name?' He looked out to sea. 'Mine is Peter Carter.'

BOOK TWO
PETER'S STORY

Strictly for the birds, Cecily, I thought, standing on that beach, waiting for you to be lying there alone.

This is all strictly for the birds.

You do think about the man who shot you. You want to go round and see him. Become his friend. Fall in love with his sister. Be discovered naked with her, by him. He naked from the bathroom, coming into her room. Or if it is a woman who shot me, I want to be naked with her brother, fucking him as she comes into the room. In a shit West Belfast two up two down. These thoughts do come to you as you lie still at night in hospital, 'fighting for your life', as they say in the newspapers, 'a soldier operating under cover and shot in Belfast last night is in a critical condition, fighting for his life'. You do no such thing, of course. You just fight, against all the odds, for one more, just one more fuck.

Right and wrong, right and wrong, wrong right, the roundelay. I was blown off the fairground ride with the moral horses going up and down. Centrifugal force, wham through the air. Into the bushes, bits of me. Down in the dirty grass amongst old coke cans, discarded wrappers. The cellulose world of weeds and rotting leaves, dark, dank, the molecular universe, where the division between inner and outer no longer applies. And you speed. Smell, hearing, all sense of scale goes. You approach a molecule. A bead, a glass planet, floating in nothingness. You stream into it. You become immensely long, strung out, you are the waves of a scream, and how long is a scream?

But desire doesn't go, even in that state. 'State?' I am talking of being near to death, death's door, Cecily. Yup. Been there. Death's door has been wide open to me. I've tiptoed right up to the edge, where the lino ends, right by the draught excluder. All I can tell you is that desire does not stop.

When I was out of coma, waking at night, putting my head up out of the miasma, I would find I had ejaculated. The nurses didn't think this was anything special.

It's common. Cripples get sexy. Immobilized by pain, you fall in love with love. A therapist explained it to me.

Strictly for the birds, though.

The birds. They come to me no longer. Understand! They weren't phantoms. They were real. They were cruel. Such cruelty must be real. I see myself lying in pain in hospital.

At night they fly down the ward to me, looping wings, big, ragged, looping in the air. Loopy birds, black falcons. Ragged feathers. Necks scrawny and pecked. They're not doing too well out there, in the night, they have their own problems these emissaries from all that savagery, in the night-time woods, over the dirty fields, scavenging for dead moles, flattened hedgehogs by the side of the motorway.

Why did they gather, night after night? I think they were there to watch me die. Since I didn't die, they settled for second best, and assembled to watch me suffer.

I'm sure it was my shoes that did for me. In Belfast, you leak what you are. No matter how much you cover up and disguise, a little of what you really are squirts away, runs in the gutter. And they notice. That I got away with it for so long amazes me. Perhaps I wasn't getting away with it all, all the time they knew this Brit was walking around their streets, their back lanes, lighting cigarettes by their walls. We know who they are, all the time, after all. And know they know us. It's all about 'containment', that is, a kind of dance, it's in a sordid dance hall called Ireland, a marathon dance that's been going on for twenty years. Sometimes there's a fight on the floor and the bouncers come in. Funny how no one thinks of shooting the band and stopping the ghastly show once and for all.

But we all need it to dance to.

They were going to put a rifle in a drain, in a back garden, off a lane. We knew that, two days ahead. The orders were to keep observation, not lift them. We were following the gun, all the way across Ireland. It had arrived with two hundred others, two months ago, on a Galway beach. We knew every hand that had touched it.

I heard them, in the lane. They were kids. One's voice hadn't even broken. It doesn't shock you at all. When you serve in Ireland you think, blow away all the kids you can. One kid down is one less hardman in ten years' time. It's an investment in the future. Of course that's how soldiers think, we are only human, and that is how I think, even now, after the pain after the birds coming for me night after night, though I doubt whether I am still

111

human. It is absurdly romantic of anyone to expect me to be.

I did, until the second I was shot, see myself as the intellectual at war. I admired T. E. Hulme's book on Classicism, there was no disgrace, the true Athenian should know the bore of a rifle barrel, how in unarmed combat to remove an assailant's eyes. The young Socrates would have done a Northern Ireland tour, perhaps the young Plato would have gone into Intelligence, undercover, like me.

But now I have been transmogrified, I am translated. I know I am done for. The attrition, an excoriation, the grinding down, the imperfection of my sorrow for the sins of the world, has utterly transformed me. I have attained a state of grace given to few. I have the right to do evil. Oh, I am so very dangerous to you, Cecily.

They were whispering. Very nervous. I knew one of them, Seamus Kennedy. He had two brothers, one dead back in '85, one in the Maze Prison. Three sisters, two were Sinn Feiners the third out of it, in Canada. A rats' nest of a little family. Seamus was the one whose voice hadn't broken. His bigger friend was carrying the armalite, under his mack, which was like a school mack, schoolboys out scrumping, just like my school mack from my grammar school uniform, back in the '50s when I'd go scrumping. And get sick eating the apples up, which were too green. Strange history, mine, for the assassin I became. I was timid and shy when I was a boy. Too bright for my own good, far too bright.

'You said you'd do it . . .', 'I'll do it . . .', 'I will if you will not,' they were arguing. Then the older of the boys took the rifle from under his schoolboy mack and said, in the way the Irish can say these things, suddenly, with the devil's rhetoric, 'A beauty. A wonder of the world.' He was quoting someone. His father? Another big brother? And Seamus took the beautiful wonder of the world, and said, 'Wait for me where we said.' 'Don't be too long about it . . .', said his companion. Seamus ran past where I stood, in my shadow. The other boy walked back the way they had come and stopped, hanging about the entrance to the lane. Seamus went into the backyard of a derelict house, further along the lane. A sack was waiting. I know, I'd looked, fifteen minutes before. After a while, he came out of the backyard and passed me. And looked at my shoes.

'Goodnight to you,' I said. And knew that was wrong. That I'd not got it right.

'Goodnight to you, Mister,' the boy said. When he rejoined his friend at the lane's entrance, they spoke a little too loudly, before they moved from earshot. 'D'you know what's on the television tonight?' 'I think it's Esther Rantzen.' 'Ah fucking Jesus . . .', and were gone. Two youngsters, common as grass, common as the litter in the streets, together for a night out.

Looking back, and I look back all the time, each grain of each second, each maverick atomic particle of time from the moment I spoke to the moment the first bullet entered me, swims in the void when I try to sleep, every scrape of my shoes, I can remember each movement of each finger, I can hear the rustle of my clothes as I moved. Yes, looking back, when I said, 'Goodnight to you', in a lane in West Belfast, it was not to a little Taig kid, small for his age, but to Monseigneur Death. He knew me by my shoes.

A profound experience is profoundly useless. It marks you with a kind of leprosy, people turn away from your terrible face. No one will look you in the eye, no one wants to listen. I've met Death in all his splendour, and wrestled with him in his doorway, and survived his embrace, closed the door on him. And it has made me a crank. I should be out in the parks in London, with the loons who talk at the tops of their voices about the tragedies of their lives, with the normal, untragic passers-by, who have the occasional catastrophe of toothache or the 'flu, turning away embarrassed. Yup! I am the Ancient Mariner come to grab your arm, Cecily, as you lie there in your swimsuit, to sing you a song you do not want to hear.

I waited. Then followed.

On the Falls Road they were talking to a woman. Shopping bag, bundle of a woman. She called out, 'Pat. How's your Mam?' The older boy, Patrick then, turned to her. I knew at once. He is going to tell her about me. I turned back. Where the fuck was my back-up car? Back-up was always dangerous, a slowing car, immediately noticed. Could not chance coming round too often. The kid was telling her, I knew . . . 'There was a man back there. In the lane. With shoes . . .' A Republican granny. Those small, gnarled women, so hard to get at, who send the generations, their sons and grandsons, to the gun. It's the mums and grans who keep the faith and the hatred of us Brits alive.

I got off the Falls. An area of rising ground, between houses, many empty.

I could feel my concentration going. I knew there was a threat, but my mind was running. There is a kind of 'dare' in the field, you dare yourself. It can get out of control. You feel you're invisible, that you are walking on water, that you can fly. The crazy sense of omnipotence has overcome officers before in Ireland, they have taken to singing Irish ballads in Republican pubs. Fear is a powerful drug, you can become addicted to its hallucinations. The moment I realized I was being followed, I was thinking . . . Empty streets. They will all leave, in the end, that is how we will win. West Belfast will be a brickfield, criss-crossed by ritual Army patrols, the odd figure like myself in civvies, standing in doorways watching dead window frames, the rooms behind them demolished. The new housing, with the back lanes twisted, that were meant to stop a terrorist running, will stand unlived in, covered by graffiti. The Catholic ghettos will be like the other side of the moon. We will visit these streets in spacesuits, to marvel. Was there once life here?

I was going to walk out onto the bypass. An R.U.C. patrol was to be parked out there, for five minutes, on the half hour. Do it that way, it was better not to be seen getting into the back-up car. It was routine, but . . .

Streets not empty. Suddenly a lot of people about. They all seem to be moving fast.

Concentrate. Get a grip. The night sky was coming down. Trapping the smells. West Belfast smells of poverty and coal fires. The sky came down, a black cloth, thick with dust, the old blackout curtains I played with in the cupboard under the stairs when I was a boy, the old gas mask which my father hated. The sodium yellow streetlighting giving the dust a sheen . . .

And I lost track. Just a second. And the streets were empty again. Only a woman on a corner, standing there, looking at me. Shopping bag. The gran the two kids spoke to? She began to raise her hand, I saw this in slow motion, her hand coming up, as if to greet me, wave me away, or wave at someone behind me . . .

'Hey you.'

And I felt a hand touch my right arm. Lightly. From behind. Hold the sleeve of my coat for an instant.

Two words. 'Hey you.' Enough.

115

In one movement I turned my pistol in my hand and shot him dead at point-blank range.

It was all in one instant, to turn, to fire, to see him die, eye to eye, at once. The round went straight through his heart.

It was the boy, Seamus.

His friend stared at me. And yes yes, an eternity does pass, in the split second. We looked at each other. Fear tore everything from me. Was I roaring? Screaming? I do not know. The fear rips all your insides out. Like a perfect vacuum, wham, sucking you away.

And his friend, the other boy, made two steps then turned to run. I shot him in the back. He spun as the round hit him, to one side. He went down, screaming, arms and legs flailing. I stepped forward, the pistol in both hands, arms straight, in an exemplary position, to shoot him in the head. Then fired.

And I rested. In time, I was in action. But remembering, being debriefed, waking screaming from nightmares, I know I rested. Like God, my work done.

But I had not fired. The fucking pistol was jammed. I slammed the weapon against the palm of my other hand. Braced, fired. Jammed again.

The woman, a distance off, was shouting.

And the sniper's bullet, to which I had been so subtly drawn, only to be interrupted by the boys so stupidly coming up to me from behind, entered my spine.

The bastards knew I was there.

It was silent. I remember nothing. I felt nothing. I heard nothing.

The bastards knew I was there.

The back-up team, who were, I was told later, beside

116

me with the car in seconds, reported that I shouted. But I have no memory of doing so.

They said I shouted, 'I am in hell.' Which was inappropriate of me. Is that not what Mr. Christian said, when he cast Captain Bligh adrift from the mutinied Bounty?

The bastards knew I was there.

I do not know if I had it at the moment I was shot, or during the days afterwards when I lay in a coma, or whether the vision is a stain imprinted into me by the neural injuries, or by chemical damage from the rush of adrenalin and fear. But I saw . . . a stretch of water. At night. Black and calm. The waters of an endless lake, not the sea, but a lake with no shore. Slowly, deep in the water, I saw the lights of all the stars. The stars were moving up to me from the depths of the lake, at first distorted and wavering but becoming clearer as they rose. Then in a rush all the stars reared up from the surface streaming with light and swirled into a vast Catherine wheel, then danced about to form the shape, beak agape dripping with starlight, of . . . a . . . huge . . . owl.

'You know what, Sir?' said the sergeant of my back-up team to me, two months after I was shot, when he came to see me as I lay in hospital. 'You know what, Sir? The bastards knew you were there.'

He was out of order. But visitors to the sick do speak out of order, in strange tones. They hear themselves and are brought up short. Hard men blushed to see me in my condition and would look down, ashamed, unexpectedly overcome.

'How do you mean, Tom?'

Sergeant Tom Baxter. Young. Tough. An iron chest, the bounds of a barrel, and a bull of a head with a strangely sensitive mouth for so perfect a soldier.

'Sir.' He wouldn't sit down.

'Sergeant, what are you trying to tell me, for fucksake!
That I was betrayed?'

I enjoyed saying that. He was near tears. I think the
birds on the rail of the hospital screen who had gathered
that afternoon approved. Rather a lot of them I remember, six or seven, three owls, two mangy kestrels, locals in
dispute about working the hospital car park and its bit of
wasteland, and two starlings tagging along, you know
what starlings are like. I say they approved. But birds
look, then look away. What do they perceive, everything
or nothing?

Baxter mumbled something and took out a silver cigarette case. Bulbous. Curling engraving upon it, an antique.
A present. Not engraved with his name of course, that
would breach security. But from him, his personal property. I think it may have once belonged to his father.

He left. The birds looked at each other with apparently
random turns of their heads, and all together flew from
the rail up into the ceiling.

Betrayed.

The migration of birds, their tittle-tattle across conti-
nents, their flocking cries for thousands of miles low over
oceans and land, is a wonder. They embrace the world
lightly, for what is lighter than a feather? Birds are everywhere. And gossips.

The bastards knew I was there. I was set up. Drawn
onto a sniper. Betrayed, Cecily.

Tempted, led, to the bullets fired by a man or a woman
I will never know, with whose sister or brother I will
never make love. Exquisitely betrayed.

Through the early days of my recovery, that certainty
saved my life. And it began with your father, the old philosopher, the spider. Yes your father. For we are related,
Cecily, not by blood but by something far more intimate.

Inevitability, my dear. The world draws tight about us. There are very few of us with any real passion, we seek each other out, criss-crossing the crowded planet, the spoiled, over-populated, revolving shit-heap we crawl across. Do we not? We are cranks who believe in fate, an elite amongst the billions of rubbish lives. We are a secret society with secret rules of love and hate.

And you lie there on the sun-drenched, tatty tourist beach, under the Greek sun, in your swimsuit, your legs lightly oiled, turning lazily to look into the haze, confident that Frank Blake, alias Frederick Wallace, alias a few other names, was your fate.

But I tell you, strictly between you me and the birds, Frank is not your fate, I am.

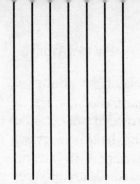

Pain. Coma. Oh England, I comb. Strictly . . .

Bullet, through right lung. Lodged in the spinal cord. Third, fourth vertebrae. Second bullet, right leg. Massive trauma.

Combed. Steel teeth. Through my blood and bone.

Combed my life out.

Two pounds ten. For a May Ball ticket. You'd think you'd get a sight of a titty, for two pounds ten.

I was in coma for three weeks. I was concussed when I went down. At first they thought the spinal damage had, in some way, got the brain. They know so little of the condition. Coma is a strange vigil. In a way you are there. You have a head of glass. You see all, but feel nothing. And you have the illusion that your life is in your gift, that you will at some time, but not now, not now, no no, not now, have to decide whether to return, up through the solid glass, to their world above of feeling and pain. The danger is, and you know it, even as you lie there in that state, that you will decide not to, you will choose to stay set in glass, the bubbles of air caught like imperfections in the hard green and bluey cold, mouth agape, to stay and be dead.

Do we have a centre at all, is there for each of us a profound, hidden 'me'?

Wrapped in us, cocooned, unseen, in the hard shell of what we appear to be, is there, wings folded, squashed, vulnerable, covered with secretions, not breathing, a secret angel?

Concussion, compaction, in the solid condition of heavy, coarse glass, there could be any shape waiting to emerge. And the trouble with angels is that their beauty fools you, you're dazzled into thinking they are wise. Like a snowy owl. While actually owls are stupid, vicious, unpredictable, the deep gaze of their eyes is a tunnel to nothing at all.

No, there was nothing in my coma. It was a vacuum. It was later, when I had climbed back up through the cold, hard, see-through rock, to scream, to give everyone a hard time, to be a bastard squirming on the sheets of my hospital bed, that I filled my time unconscious with dreams and the vivid reliving of memories.

So you invent a point. A moment when you came out of the mist and became this, 'the thing', you.

She ran across the grass at night, her shoulders bare and pure white, her ball gown of green satin in abundant folds, her shoes lost. Cambridge University. Kings College May Ball. 1964. Her name was Amanda.

And I did reinvent myself, in the months of recovery. From scratch. Out of a void. A glass head. A vacuum, full of nothing but points of light. A great labour, but necessary, for I was, that night, though I did not know it for many years, setting out to become the assassin who now approaches you in the sunshine, his stick flicking the sand, Cecily. I was unpromising material for a monster.

I was a shy grammar school boy, from a sleepy little seaside town in Sussex, an only child. My father was religious, a stalwart of the Baptist church, even when I was seventeen I still went to Sunday School. My father was a butcher, a small man, cleavering the hind legs from lambs, singing hymns. I was afraid of him when I was a

121

boy, only later did I realise he was profoundly timid. I was ashamed of my father's trade and confessed it to no one. I had found myself at Cambridge by 'rising', a star of the state system, trailing 'A' levels and school prizes. Was it of me that Lord Butler, the drafters of the 1944 Education Act, the Chartists and the dream of universal, free education, dreamt of? Me, a swot, clever, a bit of a prig? So that I could read Milton, and understand him, even understand his Latin poems, working men in the nineteenth century were chained in the hulls of transportation ships. There I was, comrades. The produce of two hundred years of egalitarian agitation, a blocked young man with a grey childhood, who would not harm a fly.

Amanda. I had not gone to the ball, of course. I was creased with lust and righteousness. Not one of them. A son of a small-town butcher? No, a son of the people, a secret enemy of the public school mouths and the rowers, the sandy-haired Olivers and Jonathans of Harrow and Winchester, Westminster School and Dulwich College. I was out of place in the early sixties. That was an England only just pulling away from the nineteen-fifties, the long boring Sunday tea time of my childhood, before the bones were rattled and the flesh was pricked by student militancy and talk of liberation.

I knew here name was Amanda. There! A drunken undergraduate runs after her, shouting it. He stumbles, he rolls, on the grass, a rugby player brought down on the field, good show, well done. He stands. He looks at me as I stand on the gravel of the quadrangle's path. The young me looks back, sober, envious. I have always been the observer, out of it, the eternal wallflower, Cecily, at life's feast, at the fucking.

'Amanda! Sorry! Please!'

She stops and turns.

From a doorway in the edifice of the college, the ancient walls, a path of light shines out over the grass. I still retain these two, my contemporaries then, but in memory harmlessly young, dewy, in their fine clothes, her gown, her white shoulders, his evening dress tie awry, his black trousers with a shiny satin stripe saggy at the knee.

'Pig! Pig! Pig!'

She runs off, through a dark gateway that leads to the backs by the river. Her suitor turns to me, swaying a little with the drink.

'I just wanted to see her titties,' he says.

'Oh,' I say.

Oh.

'Two pounds ten. For a May Ball ticket. You'd think you'd get a sight of a titty. For two pounds ten.'

'Reasonable,' I say.

He lurches. The memory lurches now, in a red mist.

'I never have!' he cries, this young upper-class milksop, back in the early sixties, what is he now, in what echelons is he lodged, within the City, the civil service or the B.B.C.? 'I never have!'

'Never have what?'

'Seen a woman's breasts.' And he blubbers. There are bubbles on his wet mouth.

'Does it matter?'

'I'm a v-virgin. Thought May Ball, fair Amanda . . . Open her bodice at dawn! Her nipples will be my first! Now what am I going to do?'

And young Peter says, 'Go and jump in the river?'

'I'll go and jump in the river,' he says and runs, turning. Forever, in the memory of that night, running and turning. The past flickers there, in perpetuity, replayed and replayed.

Pain. Coma. Oh England, I comb through.

'Thoracic chamber will flood . . . What's his name?'

This woman, white coat, with a bird's head, has a clip-board. She flicks at the page, she consults. I can hear you, perfectly, perfectly well . . .

'Christian! Christian name!'

'Peter, it's Peter . . .'

'Peter! Peter! Spit! Spit the blood out! Spit Peter!'

There is no need, at all.

'5cc. adrenalin. Cardiac resus unit . . .'

I spat. I think that at that moment when they got me to the casualty department, and I spat blood, into a curved shaped little metal bowl, held in a hard crystalline light beneath my mouth by a hard white hand, a porcelain hand, the voices of the doctors muffled by the huge bird-head masks that rested upon their shoulders, my life was saved. Spit. On you. Oh yes, then I spat. Blood pellets, stuck with feathers, against the hard metal, missing the rim and splattering the hard white flesh of a woman's wrist.

'Sh! Sh! Sh! Sh!'

Cower, for here come the boat club heavies into the college quad. Bring on the clowns, the leaders of men. They are drunk to that state when even the eyeballs seem to sweat. Evening dress all, holding onto each other, a scrum of young male muscle, a single animal with many arms and legs, going forward, back, then sideways, then collapsing in a heap. The scrum-like animal, the human beetle of youthful limbs and shiny dress shoes is con-vinced that silence is important, for it is telling itself to be quiet, 'Sh! Sh! Sh! Sh!' go its voices, fingers to lips.

No, don't cower. Don't clutch the books under my arm too tight. Put a hand in my pocket. Why am I trying to whistle? Just walk away. Just 'be' and they won't see me.

They've seen me. Oh no, no!

'Sh! Sh! Sh! Sh!'

Pink faces peek out, looking around, from the morass of limbs and arms. How I hated the look of them, the way they looked, the way they talked, the way their lips looked. Long live class hatred, I have it still. Though now, as an Ulster veteran, any one of them would be proud to buy me champagne in any club in London.

'Look! Who'sh that, over there?' . . . 'I know who that is! He's a fucking socialist!' . . . 'Show sha liss?' . . . 'Er! Er! Showsa liss fucking puke!' . . . 'Let's debag him! Let's black hish balls!' . . . 'Sh! Sh! Sh! Sh! . . .', says the beetle.

When you look back at incidents, you can recall them clearly and even, sometimes, go through them again and again, second by second. But what you forget is the fear.

I must have been very afraid. I just stood there, staring at them.

'It's fucking Harold Wilson! It is! Large as life, Harold Wilshun!' . . . 'S'not Harold Wilshun! Harold Wilshun's got bandy legs' . . . 'Shit's Harold Wilson, I can see his little pinky balls shining in the night. "Deliver me the brush of vengence!" ' . . . 'Brush!' . . .

An arm shoots up. A hand, waving a large shoe brush.

'Deliver me the boot polish of truth!' . . . 'Polish!' . . .

Another arm and hand, a tin of boot polish.

'Debag the cunt!' . . .

Here they come, 'Rurr rurr,' the pack. A loose scrum, a ruck on me, the ball. 'Nasty little man! Stop wriggling! Be a man!' Heads above me, hands mauling. The gentlemen of England, at play. They tear my trousers half down, my pants. Across my groin, scratching me, the brush, the muck of the polish is cold. I don't think about it. I go for an eye, straight, two fingers. And the pack falls away, shocked by a scream.

'My eye!' . . . 'God Jack!' . . . 'Jack's eye! He poked Jack in the eye!' . . . 'God fair play!' . . . The heavy I had caught was bent double, holding his face, whimpering. 'Gouged his eye out, has really . . . Shit!' . . .

Blood through the fingers of a hand held over a face. I used to believe in the revolution, I really did.

Oddly, I met the man I injured that night, this 'Jack', twenty years later in the bar of a Dublin Hotel. He was wearing a grey eye patch and had a sub-American accent. He worked for Hanson Trust and, with the pirate's patch and the ex-rugby player's frame still broad-shouldered, he cut a romantic figure. He was wealthy. We reminisced with no ill feeling, the assumption between us that we had both done wonderfully well. He hadn't lost an eye because of me, in drink he confessed he wore the patch for effect. It was a good story and pulled his women. So we ended up on the same side, he the captain of industry, I the secret soldier.

Dawn of the little prick.

Shouts one of them, standing back, appalled. 'Dawn of the little prick.' Yes, I am a representative of these times, I fit, my day has dawned, I am at ease, casting my shadow in the sunlight across you as you lie upon the sand.

I ran, clutching at my downed trousers.

Sh, sh. Pain. Against. Why dost thou kick?

Cervical spinal cord. Anterior nerve roots, damage unknown. Motor and sensory functions, damage. Right leg, infection present. Investigate. What tissue, nerve material lost, later. Now in coma, cannot tell the full extent of damage to motor and sensory functions, until he comes out of coma. Said the doctors, two of them both young and in white, each with a huge bird's head, he a kestrel she a kite, clipboards of notes held before them.

Why me, why me?

I hear them, I see them, up there, through the thick sea, above the surface looking way down to where I lie with the miraculous eyesight of birds of prey.

I will not come out. Up. Through the glass sea. Down here, holed down, mouth wide, water about my lips, not a bubble of air from my throat, I'll stay. Holed in memory. Why me? Why me? Why do I have to climb back up to you, out of my hole?

I will not, not, will not, not. I will not.

The great university. Your greatest days. Glory, the flowering mind.

Flower pot.

Men. Bill and. Mr. Ben Brain Damage, he do-do dumdum . . .

University of Marlowe, Milton, Wittgenstein. And what do I get? Cherry Blossom shoe polish on my balls.

Cambridge lies low, in a low landscape, on the edge of a small country town. The students have the illusion they are wandering in a rural landscape, amongst fields, a river with reedy banks, old Father Cam reverend sire, footing slow and all that. Actually it's a fen, a lowland, beset by mist, the great buildings damp, slums behind their façades, their cellars wet, the vintage wines below threatened by a rising water table, and Cambridge summer dawns are like winter. Wet with dew and cold.

'Why me?' I was thinking, shivering, my throat beginning to sore for a vicious cold.

As if by statues, by old ivy stone walls, broken columns, pedestals of sculptures that have disappeared, their inscriptions illegible, by a leaded college window in the grey stone, the room within dead and black, in mist, on a river bank from which trees lean over the still water that runs with the mist in the dim light of the early dawn,

I remember meeting your father. The landscape of a third-rate nineteenth-century romantic print mildewing on the wall of an eccentric's dilapidated house, or of the opening scene of some horror film late at night on TV, that's the memory.

Into which your father walks, Cecily. Actually along a well-kept gravel path verged by neatly mown grass. And younger than the man we know.

Oh yes! I have seen Sir Stephen Rose recently. He came to see me when I was 'rehabilitating'.

Younger, your old Dad, then. Greater speed, always just ahead of a conversation. Which he is no longer? Though he always did diverge, did he not, swing off on a tack, or as a tactic, throw a net to confuse you, the old rhetorician, the Greek dog in him keeping himself amused.

I am pausing to catch my breath. And my trousers. I have lurched in the mist, across a bridge. No one around. What to do? The massed black stickiness. Go back to my room? Will they be waiting? And he stands, the philosopher, a little way off, not upon the path, behind him, snaking into the dawn gloom, his footsteps in a curve across the glaze of dew upon the grass. A tall figure. A loose dark coat, a hat, a walking stick that he lifts and rests upon his shoulder, idly rubbing his neck with it. Very Sir Stephen, no?

'Are you drunk?' he says.

I freeze. To all students this is a great man. I had trouble with the great and good, then, I wanted to be abased, be a fool. A kind of inverted flattery, I being the one flattered.

'Debagged?'

'Yes, actually,' I manage.

He nods, gravely. 'Boat club.'

128

'Boat club,' I agree.

'We are all ritualists,' he says, relaxed, addressing the air lightly. 'Governed by ritual and habit. Against ritual and habit we break, what, perhaps twice in our lives? If we are saints that is.'

He twirls the walking stick against the collar of his coat. He muses. 'Mm,' and pauses. I stand, stained, ludicrous. And pull my trousers up, whatever the squelchy mess. Sir Stephen doesn't notice, or affects not to notice.

'Perhaps Jean-Paul Sartre is right,' he continues. 'One fears he is. Truths in moral discourse that hold water are usually crude.'

And he begins to float, his brogue shoes a few inches above the grass, he becomes opaque, I can dimly see the dark trees through him, his coat unravels into a fantastical cloak streaming out in the wind, though the dawn air is dead still, he becomes a phantom. Did this thin stuff, these eerie sentences of spectral learning, once hold me spellbound? They did. I was young. Your father, that dry old bastard, the cynic, he was my Virgil leading me down to my transformation by the fiery lake.

He continues. 'The single moment of free will, in each of our wretched existences, comes just once. And when we do not expect it. Even do not know it. At that moment we choose and live in the prison of the consequences of that choice, for the rest of our lives. Mm.'

I choose to do up the zip of my trousers but cannot.

'My zip's gone.'

'So I see,' he says, but has not looked at my crotch, has he?

He sympathises. 'Life can be bloody awful, no? Though suffering is relative. One loses, say, one's fingernails in a torture cell or . . .', waving the walking stick, with a flick of the wrist, 'one's trousers. The trouble with anguish is that it is trivial.'

A clever man, at his seminar on anguish, pain in love, literary pain.

I laugh back in his face across the years. Pain, how can I say pain? Or its words, a word like 'anguish', a phrase, 'pain's anguish'? I laugh back in his face. He can have the screams too. I say I scream. There is nothing worse, nothing, nothing, nothing.

Ha!

Ha!

Ha!

Ha!

Ha!

Ha!

But I go back down again. Sir Stephen is saying, 'I met Sartre once. A deeply pissed and aggressive little shit, I'd have thought.'

And I tug at my fly and say, 'It's torn.'

At which the teacher, the philosopher, the Socratic corrupter of youth, produces from the lapel of his jacket beneath his coat, a safety pin. He holds it out to me. I shamble forward and take it. And step back.

'Thank you very much.'

'I have a sewing needle too, loaded with thread, if that is of use.'

'Oh. Yes.'

And from his other lapel he removes a sewing needle with a length of cotton hanging from its eye.

'Old maidish of me, I know. But philosophers often are. Immanuel Kant had a rope, leading from his desk, down the stairs to the back loo. He would stand, grab the rope, and guide himself down to his bodily functions with his eyes closed, to keep his concentration.'

I am trying to fix the fly of my trousers together with the safety pin, boot polish slimy on my fingers.

'And Marx,' continues Sir Stephen, 'Marx who aimed to rebuild the world, sat for ten years upon a broken chair. Propped up by a copy of *Don Quixote.*'

'If I could take the needle back to my rooms . . .'

'But you know all about Karl Marx, don't you, Peter?'

'I'll . . . leave the needle . . . at the porter's lodge. Later.'

'Mm.' He comes nearer. 'Not the circumstances for a tutorial on the philosophy of being, eh?'

Be. Being.

'Not . . . really.'

'Be . . . ing. Funny little word.'

He looks away. The rhetorical trick of the great teacher, the great bullshitter, the manipulator, slipping in the knife. Not because he believes in anything, but because he is bored, it amuses him, it is something to do. That was why he recruited me to the S.I.S., it was something to do to start the day. It was amusing. We were in the traditional place, the backs of Cambridge University, where spies are made, the home allotment where treachery and counter-treachery are seeded. Traitors in a bean row by the banks of the river Cam. It was an amusing touch for the old man, I have no doubt. It happened to be my life, but what of that? If he'd not found me there, that early in the morning, debagged in that ludicrous state, it may never have crossed his mind to recruit me. Existentialist philosophy? Yup, Cecily. The heavy oarsman of a Cambridge boat club raises a shoe brush, thick with polish one night. Twenty-five years later, I am, therefore, standing on this beach in the afternoon sunshine.

'Dawn is always best,' says your father. 'Before you hear another human voice. It is cold. Unsullied by the warmth of others. Before the world gets muggy, the news on the radio, the postman. A little light frost on the grass, and words have a chance.'

Sir Stephen holds out the needle, the young man reaches out to take it, Sir Stephen raises his hand to make him reach higher, and says, 'You know you're going to get a first.'

I, Peter, the young man I once was, the stranger to me now, freezes.

'You're a fucking bright lad. Grammar school boy. Have you actually joined the Young Communists? You have.'

'What concern is that . . . '

'Of mine?'

The needle, the stupid needle, in his long fingers, held aloft between us, I straining to take it.

'Every concern of mine. Am I not the moral scientist? I've no patience with you, Peter! You're not cut out for class hatred. Leave that for the public school boys who attacked you tonight. The only good Marxists in this country are the upper classes. They really get stuck into class warfare. In the meantime the country has to be run by people like you, Peter. Wake up!'

My arm aching. Like some ridiculous wedding arch. Who was to walk beneath? Stuck with a great man in the middle of the backs, trying to touch his fingertips . . .

I. Eye.

'Wake up, you young fool! Choose! The choice of your life, *pace* the shitty Jean-Paul. I mean, have you?'

And he propositioned me. Civil service list, but

actually, into the Special Intelligence Services. Ah, glamour. Ah, revenge. Ah, status. Ah, self-definition. Ah, a career. Ah, a cause. Ah, identity. He would grease my way, the doors would swing open silently before me. For now, nothing to do. Get a first-class degree, a doddle, hang around the student left, keep my hand in, who the hotshots are in C.N.D., the University C.P., a doddle, ease into it, get to know the feel of never saying what you are, of being 'other' to those around you.

I took the needle. Sir Stephen turned away.

'Clean up. Breakfast in my rooms. When you've sewn up your trousers.'

He looked about his world. Light was streaming across the grass, through the trees, the grass was beginning to steam, the mist to disperse, the towers of the colleges were sharp against a clear sky. I remember he said, as he walked away, 'Early sun, I see.'

Eye. I. It is easier for the son of the lower middle classes to become a Marxist than for a rich camel to pass a needle through . . .

Easier to rise from coma, up through glass, to the eye?

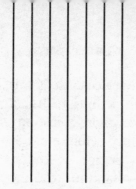

I did scream a lot. It didn't mean anything. I couldn't shake off this ridiculous hallucination that doctors had birds' heads for some time. But that went after a month or so, though, even at the rehabilitation centre, I would on a bad day get flickers of it, like a halo, a suggestion of feathers about the head of the physiotherapist. Ghostly feathers.

They tried to save the leg. Five weeks they tried. But there was so much missing. Tissue, blood vessels, nerve, half the bones in the foot. The bullet was a dum-dum, probably home-made, the end of the bullet cut into a cross with a hacksaw. An Irish cottage industry. Well, I'd say to visitors, doing the stiff upper-lip, with the unemployment so high, the Micks have got to do something over there haven't they? The effect was like a shell, shrapnel ripping everything to bits. Fortunately the round that got me in the back didn't disintegrate.

'Small mercies,' I'd say to the visitors. Ah, the visitors. I enjoyed the soldiers who came to see me, the fellow pros. My back-up Sergeant, with his father's cigarette case. The soldiers were not ashamed to say, 'There but for the grace of God . . .' Their attitude was that my wounds were fucking stupid, full stop. Their distress was frank and open, they kept their dignity. There were some officials, very ill at ease. Even the Junior Army Minister, a metropolitan smoothie, who didn't stay long. Rodney what was it, I don't recall. There was a lot of fuss about didn't stay long. Rodney what was it, I don't recall. There his visit, the doctors were flattered, hastening behind him along the corridor to my room in its glass cubicle. I had the impression he wanted to say something, but could not and left abruptly. Moved. I had the newly wounded, the fresh cripple's contempt for the healthy who find themselves 'moved' at the sight of what they insultingly call 'your bravery', or worse, 'your brave suffering'. And there was my father. Small, round bellied, no longer really a fat man, beginning to shrink in old age, his flappy brown suit too big for him. He sat on the tubular hospital chair not knowing what to do with his hands. His pale eyes watery, the whites yellowing, in their grief had no depth. I knew his anguish at the sight of me made him tremble, he had no resources to deal with it. 'My old boy,' he kept on saying, 'How are you, old boy?' And, 'Oh my poor old boy.' He made no attempt to pray with me, he made no religious reference, he did not bring me a testament. He did not bring my anything at all, what could he? After a while he stood and kissed me on the face, the first time he had done that since I was what, thirteen? Then we went away. For an hour I wept uncontrollably.

And the leg. Anyway, the fucking leg got the soldier's friend. Queen Gangrene. All the antibiotics of the modern world, still they cannot keep her away. She will get into the hospital, late at night, to kiss the soldier's wounds. They could have gone on trying. Cut the infected bits away. Built a cosmetic leg, some of the real me mixed up with bright pink plastic. Moulded, with a bunchy little calf muscle at the back, like an athlete. But I would have had pain all the time, especially in bad weather, I would have been lodged in a very particular circle of hell, that of wounded soldiers with cosmetic legs, in perpetual English weather. So I said to the Gods . . . 'Amputate.'

There is a luxury of horrendous injury in the hours of boredom, the half-sleep under the painkillers, the weakening of your body in the bed, always warm, always clean with the attentions of the nurses, a perpetual state of fever floating there. It is the luxury of total self-obsession. You practise a seamless daydreaming. You do a lot of travelling, over deserts, snowfields, river banks in spring, you know, dreams of freedom. Sometimes as you slide along you can turn over and look down and see yourself, lying asleep in the snow or in the grass.

So I calmed. There was no doubt that I had been betrayed in Belfast. But I could not maintain the anger, through the long half-good days, the bad days. After three months of the hospital, I was moved to Tring, in Hertfordshire, a rehabilitation centre. A big house, redbrick, of some obscure former glory. There were still some Falklands lads there. A world of its own, ping pong played in wheelchairs, echoey rooms, physio sessions on gym mats beneath high moulded ceilings of elaborate and leafy plaster, rushes of tomfoolery amongst the patients, laughter and japes, smuggling alcohol in, on one weekend the stowing away of two London whores in a loft room, the girls discovered stoned and asleep in each other's arms by an outraged matron on her morning rounds, and the routine days of depression, the smell of incontinence or ruined young men's bodies, of Jeyes cleaning fluid, of kitchen meals, two veg and custard on treacle pudding, the long winter days of rain upon tall windows.

'Being institutionalised' is a condition that is obvious from the outside. When you are inside it you can do nothing about it. It's an addiction. It is shameful to say, but I became dependent upon being a cripple. I had been betrayed, for a time I raged. But my anger leached away. My tantrums became petty. What do they mean, no spotted dick for pudding tonight? There's always spotted dick on Tuesdays! What the fuck is going on! What the fuck do they mean, jelly and ice-cream? It's Tuesday! I embraced by victimhood. The rug across my knees in my wheelchair became my emblem. I became gentle, I only mildly fussed. The rug must be folded at each corner and tucked, thus. Thus. No other way.

I had come to accept that I would never walk again. The doctors and I entered into a conspiracy between us. We kept up the fiction, with agonising physio sessions, special instructors in track suits, two fit young men, both Scots, bending me on the massage tables, encouraging profuse sweating on the gym mats, with a mixture of infinite politeness to my rank, age and experience, blended with foul language. 'Y' can fuck this one Sir, I'll have y' sucking y'self off Sir, no time at all Sir, ye'll be amazed, just give me a little of your patience Sir.' But the spine, the spine. Something was torn. Paralysis came and went, tearing cramps of muscle against muscle, numbness and pain threaded down my back in streaks into what was left of my legs. It was a ritual for the hero, for in this enclosed world I was a great man, I was James Bond, glamour radiated from my wounds and flew banners from my wheelchair as I passed along the corridors. Whispers, 'Shot in Ireland. Under cover.' When I left Tring for 'the outside', your real world, to sit in a pub, a cripple growing old in the corner of the saloon bar slobbering a pint, I would be, what? Piteous. Bloated with paraplegic fat. I'd need 'special care', I avoided discussing it. I never wanted to leave, I did not discuss it, I kept up the pretence of a heroic struggle at the parallel bars.

But one doctor wanted me to face the truth of my condition, to embrace my predicament. And, 'Along life's way', that old Baptist Church phrase, 'Along life's way' you do meet these souls that are in love with reality and burn with a zeal for you to embrace it. What a pain in the arse they are.

Her name was Juliana, Dr. Juliana Moore. Tall, long brown hair, owl-hazel eyes, high cheek bones, something South American about her good looks, Inca, a finely chiselled nose, a small mouth which she would usually leave pale and mean but now and then would lipstick with an orangey red. Juliana. I did, for a while, believe she loved me. But the relationship between the mutilated patient and the whole and healthy physician is dodgy, very dodgy, the stuff of wet dreams, on my part if not hers. She wasn't army, she was a civilian specialist, a psychiatrist, something about the trauma of the wounded. She spent a year with a unit at the Royal Naval Hospital, Haslar, Gosport, treating sailors damaged, 'traumatised', oh the jargon, in the Falklands. She and I fought from the start. Trauma? 'Give me all the screaming heebie-jeebies and mental scars you like, if you give me back my leg . . .', 'You think I am a vegetable, don't you . . .', 'Dr. Juliana, don't you want me to get up and walk? . . .' I would say to her. Professional distance, there, I was the case study, the notes for a future article in a learned medical publication. On the delusion of the traumatised? The passivity of the victim? I played the boor, the philistine, to try to direct her observer's, her recorder's indifferent gaze.

'There is someone to see you.' It was nine in the morning, in the big room at the back of the house on the ground floor, with the parallel bars, along which I was to struggle to walk in the regular charade. The windows were slatted with Venetian blinds, closed against eyes prying from outside on the agony of those who groaned and hauled their broken bodies within the room. In smart Adidas track suit, silver grey, all the gear, artificial limb strapped on, I was being held on either side by the two Jock physios. Juliana came in. 'There is someone to see you.'

'Easy Sir . . .', said a Jock.

I had a sudden dread. 'Who?'

She looked at me. She shifted her weight, a sexy stance it seemed, deliberate. She was assessing me, as she always did. Judging. Juliana, lady of pain.

'Fuck you! Who?' I shouted.

'Sir Stephen Rose.'

The Jocks didn't like it but I stood, between the two bars, propped up. Track suit, white towel about my neck, upon my feet, one real one false, gleaming white Reebok trainers. A broken icon. And I got them out of the room. And stood there, beginning to sweat, the strain on my arms . . . Brace, balance, don't crumple before the bastard.

I had not seen him for twenty years. My mentor, my corrupter, my recruiter. I knew of his influence, the touch of his hand in security matters, his 'grey eminence' legend, but I had avoided any reunion and none was sought by him.

And he walked into the room. Less boney. Ah, drink. The don's tipple getting to him, the port, the whisky of a night while unable to sleep? Insomniac as ever. Does he still patrol the backs of Cambridge colleges, looking for lonely, lefty students to pervert, to send to war? Yes, much older. A coloured shirt, a brown coat of bristly wool. Much older, serrated puffs of skin beneath the eyes.

He stood, looking at me, the figure in immaculate

139

sportswear, in-between the bars of the apparatus, what, like a Francis Bacon painting, humanity smeared? For I felt the slew of my body, the unnatural angle of my feet.

He had his hands in his coat. He took a breath, drawing himself up to something of his former height, about to pronounce.

'Shut up you fucker!' I shouted at him. And got him in one. I saw his mouth set.

I slammed my hands and forearms upon the bars. I yelled and slung my dead half-leg forward. I yelled again and got my whole leg before it. I yelled, lunged hands and forearms forward, yelled, got another step, my chest felt as if it had a hard, hot boulder lodged within it, the rib bones and flesh taut to bursting, I yelled again and held myself still, panting. 'How many steps have I done?'

'I . . .'

'Don't fuck me about! How many fucking steps?'

'Two,' he replied, his voice barely audible.

'I said don't fuck me! How many?'

'Two!' He paused. 'Two steps. I . . .'

'Wait!' and I threw myself, sideways, making my whole body leer, into another step. 'How many?'

'Three . . . If you do not want me here . . .'

'We scream and yell a lot in this place. It doesn't mean anything.'

'No?'

I knew I couldn't unsettle him forever. That was what I wanted to do. To embarrass him, humiliate him with my deformity, not give him an inch, to fling my wounds in his face until he sank to his knees with his mind destroyed.

'What did you say?' I spat at him.

He paused. Getting the drift of what I was up to. The

old mandarin's mind was still intact and deadly. Looking back on the encounter in the following days, I realised I knew that he would get the better of me, that it would be I upon my knees, bereft of all self-respect and self-control.

'I said, if you do not want me here while you . . ., and he made a slight gesture at the parallel bars.

'While I walk?' I relaxed, as best I could, my good knee locked. 'Not up to me. We, the great unlegged, give up a number of human rights. Among them the right to say who will or who will not visit us, lump us about, give us chocolates, grapes, wheel us in or out of the sun. Who the fuck asked you to come, anyway?'

'You did,' he said.

'Did I?'

'Repeatedly, so I was told.'

He was fighting back.

'When I was delirious, do you mean? Does that count?'

'I stayed away until I was advised . . . that you were fit enough.'

'Advised by whom?'

'Doctor . . . Moore is it?'

'Ah.' A whiff of rodent. So this was Juliana's idea? Part of the course toward the reality of my lot on earth? 'She asked you here? The cunt with the long brown hair?'

'She said . . . the time was ripe.' An edge of contempt was asserting itself in his voice.

'You know,' I said, unable to stop myself boasting about my injuries, 'the round that got me in the back didn't disintegrate?'

'Small mercies,' said Sir Stephen.

'You bet.'

An own goal, mentioning one of the bullets. I slapped the palms of my hands on the bars and said, cod, in zummerzet, 'Anyway! Can't stand here all day nattering to the likes o' you, I got to get on down his hill, down to the lower meadow.'

But I could not move. 'Am I giving you a hard time, Sir Stephen?' I managed to say.

'Not as hard as you are giving yourself.'

'Ah. Ah.' I rested.

'Does . . . my admiration for your sheer bloody guts do any good at all?'

'None at all.'

He looked away and at the windows blocked by the white blinds, to say, 'Whereof we cannot speak . . .'

What was this? The old cove getting sentimental? Had the bastard become a drippy mystic?

I completed the quotation. '. . . Thereof we must remain silent.' I blew out a lungful of air, the cramps going. I had found a position of relative comfort on the bars, that was all that mattered.

'Well,' I said, 'Wittgenstein did write that in the trenches. First World War. A lot of de-legging going on. But,' I shook my head, 'no. Nothing. Your "admiration" gives me not a tickle. If I shouted out your name while I was delirious, asked for you to be brought . . . out of the woodwork? Perhaps it was because you recruited me. In the end, you sent me to Belfast. To the bullets.'

The old man seemed to tremble. Had I got him? Had I really got him?

'Oh I dreaded this,' he said.

'Not to accuse you,' I said.

'This I dreaded.'

I was startled. What was this? Genuine feeling? Remorse, even? From my Frankenstein? Who had taken a shy innocent and made me? It was unbearable. Anger

142

tore into me. 'If I did ask for you,' I said, 'it was just . . . for completeness. Look!'

I lunged forward, twisting to lurch another step. But my left hand slipped from the bar. I fell to the matting beneath, feeling a blaze in my right shoulder as a muscle tore. 'Fuck! Fuck! Fuck!' I yelled.

'God, Help him someone! Doctor!' cried Stephen in great distress, turning. I saw he was making for the bell by the door to summon help.

'Don't touch that!' I shouted from the floor. 'Don't you! Don't get the birds' heads in here, the Gods! Don't have anything to do with them!'

He stood still. Then turned and looked at me.

'I'm all right,' I said. 'I throw myself about all the time, it's nothing.'

A silence between us. I lay where I had fallen.

'I will be honest,' he said. 'When the hospital contacted me and said you wanted to see me, I was embarrassed. I couldn't remember who you were.'

He paused. I let him.

He sighed. 'But I asked around, feelers, I learnt of your operation. The door of the sanctum is still open to me. I was an Intelligence Officer, in the war. I did rather well in North Africa. They made me a Colonel and brought me back home. I was in the same room as Eisenhower in a country house in Hampshire, when he decided the date for D-day. After the war I went to Palestine. I have seen many men in your predicament, many.'

Sorrow, a cloud of sorrow hung about him. This was all wrong! Was I to pity him, not he me?

'Then after the Palestine disaster, I returned to Cambridge. My academic career took off, but I still had the itch. They say you never leave the Secret Services.

Nor do you. You still scratch. The conspiratorial itch.'

I could not allow this, I could not! 'I see,' I said. 'So you wandered around Cambridge at dawn, perverting the young.'

'I kept my eyes open. To see what I could pick up.'

Then I propped myself up on an elbow. 'A philosopher scratches himself. Twenty years later I lose a leg. There's a kind of comfort there. In the absurdity. I'll be all right now.'

Everything was at peace. I had diminished him. He hesitated, then said, 'If there's anything I can do, anything I can get you . . .'

'How about some hard pornography?'

'Surely.'

'It does hit you. Lust.'

'Of what predilection?'

'Oh, nurses? Going down on cripples' cocks?'

'I'll . . .' He nodded.

I looked across the yellow wooden floor of the room at him, an eminent man in a brown overcoat. I could have scuttled as a mouse toward his shoes.

'You know that you were betrayed,' he said.

The parallel lines of the narrow boards of the floor, a gymnasium floor, ran clean to the white wainscot of the white wall. Why didn't he take that coat off? It was warm in the room. Did it reassure him that at any moment he could leave the sickly hothouse and walk back into the winter drizzle outside?

'That has not occurred to you?'

I should have spat at him, forced him away there and then, crawled at him snarling, a madman screaming spittle at him, dragging myself by my elbows across the floorboards like a lunatic in the snake pit of an eighteenth-century asylum. But I could not move. He could have walked to where I lay and crushed my head with his shoe.

'Peter, I need your forgiveness.'

The torn muscle in my shoulder sang. I remember thinking, concentrate on that. Then he won't say what he has come to say.

'Doubly betrayed. S.A.S. Special Intelligence was warned that your cover was blown.'

'No,' I said, though I knew it had to be true the second he said it.

'Warned by a very powerful source.'

'No. No.'

'Let me do this for you, please.'

'For me?' I snapped at him. 'You mean to me.'

'I must tell you.' He looked down. 'Special Intelligence decided not to pull you out. They decided to continue with the operation, and leave you in the field.'

'No.'

'They did so to test the source of the information. To see if he was any good. To . . .', he faltered. 'To see if anything would happen to you. It is a very powerful source. Of great . . .', again he faltered. I realised that he was near to tears. 'Great . . . potential.'

'Potential.'

'Yes. Great potential use.'

'So . . . If I got shot, they would know this "source" was good.'

A silence.

'Yes.'

Lightheaded, I felt light, the syllables of our words seemed tinsel, blown about in the breath it took to send them into the air.

'And . . . What?' I said. 'Since I am lying here, like this, this informant, this "source", is now treasured?'

'I should not have told you,' said Sir Stephen, looking away, his face now streaming with tears. 'I have breached my trust.' He paused, then said, in a strange voice, 'But it is all, one might say, all in the family.'

My country had thrown me away.

'And whose vile scheme was this?'

'He came to see you.'

The Metropolitan smoothie? About whose visit, early on in my recovery there had been all the fuss? Yes, yes of course. Some Rodney, the Junior Army Officer? No wonder he had seemed see-through, a perspex man, an 'I am not here, do not see me'.

'Ireland has . . . distorted all our thinking,' said Sir Stephen.

'Distorted our bodies, you mean.'

'The impasse, the . . .' he faltered. What could he not bring himself to say? 'The morality? The impasse has distorted our morality?' I despised him. How dare he suffer conscience, how dare he feel tears in his eyes while standing in a gymnasium electric with the pain of the wounded.

'You know what you have done to me?' I said. 'You have forced me to walk again. You bastard.'

Oh Daddy, Daddy, I know you love me, take your poor boy in your arms and rock me, hold my head, I've got a cold, hold my head and I'll go to sleep.

'I'd made my peace, Sir Stephen. I knew I was set up. But not like that! Not . . . by England itself . . .'

'Peter, please, I . . .'

'Made my peace! I was going to sit in a chair. Be a cripple. Wheeled out into the sun.'

Would I never rid myself of innocence? Would I always be the only child, from nowhere?

'I was cut off, cleanly. But now you come to me . . .'

The torn muscle in my shoulder was warming. Heat began to radiate through my body.

An angel enfolded, the creak of wings within the chrysalis.

My hatred was beginning to stir.

'Who is he?'

A silence.

'This "source". This golden goose? Who is worth my spine, my leg? Who is valued more than me, more than a soldier, for whom you threw me away? Tell me!'

'I said!' Sir Stephen shouted, in distress. He breathed, then spoke quietly. 'I said, all in the family. His name is Francis Edward Blake. He is, by the fates, also my son-in-law. I have a wayward daughter.'

Frank Blake. Oh absurdity, laughter, jackanapes.

'You know I am out of line here, Peter . . .'

'I was sacrificed for that man?'

Jackanapes, old crow, ragged, bust wing, low over the motorway, hit by a windscreen at a hundred miles an hour, scruff feathers, cracked beak, scarecrow, a dead joke. I began to laugh.

'. . . Right out of step to tell you this, I do so . . . out of conscience.'

'What code name has he been given?'

'Frederick Wallace.'

'Wallace? "W" category? Is he that hot?'

'There are they who think so.'

'And he fucks your daughter?' And I laughed at him, I laughed at his face, now red with weeping and distress, I laughed, feeling the warmth increasing within me, the heat. 'All in the family! It's just a few of us. A few policemen a few politicos, a few soldiers, all locked in a room. Blood on the walls, beating each other to a pulp. Eh? Eh Sir Stephen? A locked room we dare not leave.

Because we love it so. I do believe I love it so, even lying here like this. I love it, I'd give my life to it, I half already have. I love the . . . the . . .'

And he said it. 'The terror.'

'Yes, philosopher. In our bloodstained room. While out in the street real life goes past? Ordinary people, unaware of the horror behind the curtains. The beatings, the human flesh forced down the toilets. Right?'

The blood hissed in my ears. Sweat seeped from me, my clothes were sodden.

I swivelled on my left knee. I got both hands on a bar. I pulled myself up in one, the bar beneath my ribs. Sing! Sing! Sing, pain!

I extended my arms. The torn muscle howled. With the jackknife manoeuvre of a high diver I twisted with a shout and had my hands on either bar.

'Go!' And I lunged forward, slapping my hands and forearms before me and took a step. 'Go!' I took another. I turned on Sir Stephen. 'Go! I said Go!' I shouted at him.

He turned and left, closing the door softly.

I stood alone between the wooden bars of smooth mahogany. They were stained with sweat to a deep dark red.

Sing!

I got to the end, five steps, before they rushed into the room as I collapsed and blacked out.

I decided three things. When I could walk again I would always wear a black suit. I would carry a stick, not because I would need to, but to honour my disability. And I would kill Frank Blake.

Not Sir Stephen, not this Rodney, not the grey, hidden men.

Frank Blake.

The Rodneys will always be there, in the offices, in the background. With little flags on maps.

The automatons. They are already dead, have you noticed that so many are, Cecily? So many were dead from the moment they were born, though they may walk around for seventy or more years.

Or they die along the way, like your father. He did in Palestine. He tried to tell me, but I wouldn't let him.

What revenge is there, to kill one of the Rodneys? One of the grey, walking dead?

But Frank, ah, that is a different order. Frank stands amongst the order of angels, for he actually is . . . alive.

The Rodneys let me be shot, they left me on the streets of hell, for the snipers' bullets. To test Frank's word, to see if he was the real thing.

And Frank is the real thing. Is he not, my dear? You must know. I bet he fucks you good.

Does he fuck you good?

Oh yes. He's one of the few, he is one of the living, all right. That is why I pursue him. It is beyond 'tit for tat', it is beyond revenge. It has no logic, but matters of life and death are not logical, are they? Is your love for the bastard 'logical'?

And here I am, Cecily. In black. With stick.

I am very pure. I am pure . . . will.

How strong is 'the human will'? How far into you can you send it? How deep into the stuff of the cells of the body itself? By will, I suspect you can rearrange the DNA code within you if you are dedicated enough, ferocious enough, if you give yourself utterly to one idea, like a sacrifice on a pagan alter to the stone knife. But you must be pure, you must be ruthless, you must have one single desire.

And I did.

I demanded everything from the two Jock physios in my programme of recovery. Our roles were reversed, I bullied them to more and more effort. One of them, a decent young man, broke under the strain of my demands. I had no sympathy. I snapped him in two and threw him away. His breakdown drove me on with a terrible glee. After a day's workouts and exercises, baths and massages, pummellings and screamings, torturings in the clutches of the chrome and steel and sweated leather of the gymnasium's machines, I studied the physiology of my condition. I revised their programmes for my recovery. I appalled everyone around me.

But I became pure. And I walked.

'I feel you blame me,' I said to Juliana a few days before my discharge. It was spring. We walked across the lawn toward rhododendron bushes and trees.

'How can that be?' she said.

'I don't know,' I said.

'If you want some counselling, it is easily arranged . . .'

'Don't be fucking stupid,' I said. Remade. Indeed, truly self-made. In black. With stick.

She stopped. 'Look,' she said, 'I am a technician.'

'Butcher?'

She was angry.

I kept at her. 'That was my father's trade. The legs of little baby lambs. You're one of the butchery team? Psychiatry, you slice the mind up, no? Put in bits of metal, plastic joints. Into thoughts, not flesh.'

She walked on. 'Yes, if you like. We do our butcher's cuts, then hope nature will do her work. And heal our crude interventions.'

'Then why,' I said, 'are you choked with resentment? Why do you hate this . . . testament to your skill, upright on one and a half legs? This artistically rearranged artefact? Because the meat under the knife thinks too much?'

'This is not a conversation to have with a patient. I think I will end it.'

I was getting to her. I wanted this one, I wanted some of the shrapnel of me lodged in her, to suppurate after I had gone.

'I shouldn't be walking about, should I? You didn't expect it. You had me down for a vegetable. The cabbage should not have grown legs again. Is that it?'

We entered the shade of the bushes and trees. Spring, at the edge of the grass there were primroses. But under the rhododendrons there was just earth and dried remnants of foliage, sour plants, nothing can grow near them.

'I don't know,' she whispered.

'What? What?'

She looked me full in the face. Hazel. Dense eyes. Intelligence there, health. I hated her.

'We don't know, Peter,' she said. Using my name. The bitch still disliked me. Even held me in contempt. I'll cut that out, I thought. 'It seemed that the neurones, the electric connections if you like, in the damaged part of your spine were just not there anymore. But you've healed . . .'

'You mean by faith,' I said.

She paused, then said, 'Or by hate'.

'What?'

'You heard.'

Juliana, clever owl woman, clever head, you looked right through the dark and right through me.

'You've decided there's someone you hate,' she went on. 'That's why you've recovered.'

I laughed in her face and said something about her

trite, therapist's mumbo-jumbo. And she was right, of course. But it'll be all right, I thought, I'm going to wear black, no one will be able to see through me, ever again.

Then she said, quietly, looking down, 'Is it me you've decided to hate?'

So wrong there! And, suddenly, so vulnerable. So easy to hurt.

'When I was in fever, after I came out of the coma, feverish with the gangrene . . .', I began.

She shook her head. 'No, I . . .'

'. . .You seemed like gods, all you doctors.'

Shaking her head. 'No.' Then she said, 'You must be careful. A blow, to your spine, you could be far worse. You do know that? You have understood that?'

'Will you do something for me?' I said. I knew she would. I paused, then said, with no smile, with nothing in my voice, 'Will you show me your breasts?'

She hesitated, she turned away, she turned back to me. She lifted the pink jersey she was wearing above her sensible skirt. She let it fall to the earth. She unbuttoned her blouse and pulled it back on her shoulders. She reached up behind her shoulder blades and undid her bra, then pulled the strap off her shoulders. Her beautiful breasts looked at me, the nipples large and pitted, the curve of their fullness pronounced by the side of her arms, which I saw were slender, her skin pale brown shaded by the dappled sunlight under the trees. She looked down, standing utterly still. Then, unhurried, at the same pace she had undone them, she closed her bra and buttoned her blouse. Then she looked me full in the face.

'Do you forgive me for that?' I said.

'No,' she said.

I was exultant, I was glad. I had destroyed anything,

any flicker of feeling she may have had for me. I was pure and straight for my quest.

'Why not? Ah, come on Juliana. What about pity? "Pity"?'

She held her stare straight into my eyes. 'I think everything you stand for is unforgivable.'

'Except my life. You saved my life.'

'You will die soon enough,' she said and walked away.

I watched her go.

Contra natura.

Is the DNA itself against nature?

We revolt creation itself, which works with a kind of yearning to return to inert chemicals, the purity of a desert on Mars, dead, irradiated, lifted by thin winds at a hundred and fifty miles an hour. That is the harmony creation desires.

Not us.

Not this miasma, the blocked chaos of living cells.

Not this mutilated creature, Peter Carter, neurones precariously regrown, scar tissue glowing, humiliating a woman amongst dark rhododendron bushes.

Contra natura, not what nature had in mind at all.

All the angelic beings, the imaginary birds of my days and nights of suffering, the hallucinatory creatures that rose from the molten glass of coma, beads of glass strewn about the sky, the torn feathers with dark blood upon their quills, died for me as I watched her walk away. I had a last, fleeting vision of them. They had been born in my mind and had shone with a light of their own. They died like the sparks from a burning piece of paper, their extinction so quick the eye could hardly follow. I had been held in a spell. They had appeared on the charmed

153

horizon and flown toward me. So real! Then they fell back into chaos.

And I was left, the manner of thing you see before you, Cecily.

BOOK THREE
TO THE WHOREHOUSE

'But what is in a name?' He looked out to sea. 'Mine is Peter Carter.'

The precision with which he had said both their real and their false names froze Cecily. He spoke them as a news reader would announce the names of the dead in a plane crash or a railway accident, with respect but with a hint of knowingness, an unctuous tone.

A death professional?

I am about to be very, very afraid, she thought.

Peter Carter.

The name Frank had given her in prison.

The name that was like a witch's spell, that she had whispered to her sister, that had put Frank onto a London bridge with a junior member of the Government.

This was the man who had the name.

Yes. I am about to be to be terrified. With his appearance in the noonday heat something had happened, she knew that the world had taken a shift, that life had in some awful way crumpled, and was turning inside out. She lay dead still.

Peter Carter squinted. 'The one with Frank, out on the raft. That must be the brother.'

Cecily saw that his boyish face was etched with lines, crow's-feet at his eyes and creases into his cheeks from the corners of his mouth. A gargoyle, half human, half animal, on a church in stone, looking ahead for ever.

'Oh Cecily,' he said, 'have you enjoyed playing the gangster's moll?'

I must turn over, she thought, I cannot bear this horrible man standing above me. Lying there, she felt vulnerable, stretched out on her back, his feet a yard from her head. But she could not bring herself to turn, she could not time it, she had to keep still. This was an apparition. She was dreaming. The black-suited figure with a stick towered up above her into the blue sky. The fear was working through her fast, a paralysing poison. Before this man in black she felt as if she were strapped down upon a table before a libertine, or a cruel tattooist about to disfigure her with needles. Against her will she was startled by the rush of sexual response within her.

'Frank looks fit,' he said. 'Drinks like a fish but keeps lean. Deprived childhood? I know men from the Belfast slums on ten thousand calories a day of booze but . . .' He hit his stomach with his free hand. 'Stomachs like the north wall of Eiger.'

Paralysed, poisoned, he could lean over and pour the poison down my throat.

'The brother is a slob though,' continued Peter Carter. 'Be careful of the brother, Cecily. You find him a slob? The concept of the working-class body beautiful breaks down there.'

With an effort she forced herself to turn over. She knelt up to confront him.

'At least Frank is a real man,' she said. Meaning, I know you are not, that beside Frank you are a freak, weakling, you are dead, a walking corpse in the world of the living and the sexually alive.

'A real man,' he said, with a sarcastic edge. 'An old-fashioned phrase, from a modern woman like you.'

She sensed disease, dangerous sickness, a psychotic fire in him. Repulsion pushed at her from this Peter Carter. It was horrible to be near him. Frank, come out of the water. Frank. Now.

'A real man,' he repeated and smiled, ashen, weary, but relaxed, confident in some hideous strength within him. 'And what am I? A beach pervert?'

Cecily tried to slam the shutter down on him at once. To cut him. As you have to cut men who come up to you on a late-night railway station, having a cup of tea in a London park, anywhere. The woman's predicament, to be forever on your guard, guillotining the space between you and strange men.

'If you know about Frank, you know about his temper,' she said, with all the contempt she could muster. 'He will not take kindly to you talking to me.'

'No he will not,' said Carter. 'At all,' and smiled again.

Say I know nothing of Frank's life, say I am nothing to do with it, threaten him. 'I mean it. I am married to a violent man.'

'You like that, do you? Does he knock you about? In bed?'

Anger flashed through her, making her jump it was so strong. 'I think you should go away,' she said quietly, almost hissing.

157

'Mm,' said Carter, flicking the sand with his stick. 'I don't think you know about your husband's violence, Cecily. Indeed, I don't think you know anything about your husband.'

He's trying to make everything dirty. That's what he's doing. What was awful, she realised, was that he was succeeding, the poison was slimy, a mucus flowing from him all over her.

And then he was suddenly talking fast, a jabber, spat out at her with a vicious intensity.

'Have you any idea what your Frank is doing? That he is trying to play a double game with the British Security Services and the I.R.A.?'

He scoffed, a half laugh from his throat, like a vicious little cough.

'Like he is playing a game, in some school playground? Our own side is pretty nasty, I do assure you. But do you have any idea what the Irish hardmen are like, what they do? Even to their own kind? Shall I tell you about an I.R.A. punishment squad?'

She found herself trying to give as good as she got, to spit words back, overlapping him as he spoke. 'Don't try to frighten me, don't you, you won't get between us. You won't have us . . .'

'He does jobs for those animals, Cecily.'

'. . . No, no, I don't want to talk to you . . .'

'. . . Their creature. He robs for them, Cecily . . .'

'. . . No . . .'

'. . . Then he sells us information. Who set the robberies up, where the money went, names, places. Three jobs we know about, since you married . . . The last one a post office, little post office in Dundalk . . .'

'. . . Nothing you can say . . .'

'. . . The postmistress, she was an old woman, they tied

her up, and knocked her about, kicked her. She got glass
in her eye . . .'
'Nothing . . .'
'. . . Kicked her while she was tied to her chair, a bottle
was smashed . . .'
'. . . No . . .'
'. . . Probably Brian getting out of hand, but Frank uses
his brother to get out of hand, have you noticed that? . . .'
'. . . No, no, Frank would never . . .'
'. . . The old woman got her hip shattered, tell you of
that did he? Boast of that, in bed? . . .'
'. . . Who are you, what are you, why are you saying
these things? . . .'
'. . . Boast of beating up a poor old Irish woman while
you lay in his arms . . .'
'. . . What do you want, what . . . ?'
'. . . No he doesn't tell you anything, does he, but you
know. You know, Cecily . . . In your heart, you know
what he is . . .'
'. . . I asked you, who, what are you? . . .'
'. . . He is even less than the scum he is mixed up with.
On the human scale. And it can go down very very low,
the human scale, way below zero . . .'
Covered in the vile mucus, sticking to her, heavy on
her arms, glueing her fingers, her eyes, '. . . You don't
know anything about Frank, you don't know about his
life, you don't know about his . . .' She hesitated. He had
stopped spitting the words at her, the vile things. She was
going to say, 'You don't know about his beauty.'
'I don't know about his what?' He paused. 'What were
you going to say?'
She was silent.
'Were you going to say that I don't know about his
beauty?'

Ice touched her, deep inside. A knife of ice. What is this evil?

He was not looking at her. His gaze was out to sea. His manner, after the spate of words between them, had become casual, soporific, even off-hand. He was sleep-walking, half in a dream. With a jolt Cecily sensed what was happening. He was run through with pleasure. This was intolerably sweet to him. Revenge, this is revenge to him she thought, appalled.

He paused, then said, 'Frank gave you my name in prison. Did he not. And you gave it to your sister? So Frank could meet someone? The grey Rodney?'

Cecily flinched. This man knew everything. Invisibly, had he always been there, from the moment Frank was released? Was he a ghost, who had been in the cottage, the first time they made love, in the corner of the little bedroom with the floral wallpaper, in the bushes of the night-time garden?

A mad thought. She remembered the bird that had crossed the lawn before them, that night, while they huddled in each other's arms. Had the bird been this man's spy?

Mad.

'Yes, I do know a lot about you, Cecily,' he said.

Could he read her thoughts? Could this apparition pass through her head?

'I was well trained at my trade, you see.' He sighed. 'My wretched trade. It is falling apart, it has lost its way, badly.'

'What trade?' She wanted to shout at him, to swear at him, but dare not. 'What trade?'

He paused.

'Ah, England. Do you love England? We come from a country of old Victorian sewers, collapsing, under our feet but out of sight. Our security services are very similar. Rotting sewers, loose bricks and rats, but out of sight'.

She realised that she was kneeling. She was kneeling before him, a suppliant.

'I work for England, Cecily. For England in Ireland. In your left-wing days, did you talk of the power of the state? Did you rail against "The English secret police"?'

He made an ironic little bow to her, stiff from the waist. 'Meet the real thing.'

'Don't hurt us,' she heard herself say. 'Please don't hurt us.'

Peter Carter took a slow breath.

'What do you know of "hurt", Cecily? What can you possibly know?'

And he looked her in the eye for the first time. In the sorrow of the way he had spoken she felt again the rush of a repulsive sexuality between them. What now? Was she, kneeling before him, to loosen his fly and take him in her mouth, to placate him? To be struck down in the sand by his stick, which he would, when he had had his way in her mouth, raise in the Greek sun against her? She shivered, revolted, trying to brush the thought from her as she would an insect from the skin of her shoulder.

'The information about you is that you messed about on the left in London. C.N.D.? Gay rights? Joined the Labour Party nineteen eighty-three because of Benn, left nineteen eighty-five because of Kinnock.'

'Information? What do you mean, the "information about me"?'

He smiled.

This man has bought my soul, she thought, in a shop, in a sordid shop, in Ireland, in a London backstreet, and I did not know it was even lying there, for sale.

'You have dabbled, Cecily. Dabbled.'

'Yes,' she said. 'Yes, I have.'

'And now you are on this beach. With kisses from this filth all over you.'

She jerked back.

'Don't get up,' he said. 'Just stay still. There is just one little thing I want to say to you, before your husband comes out of the sea.'

Why did she obey? Why did she do exactly what he said? She hated herself. His effortless, terrible authority. He has my soul in his pocket. It is heart-shaped, it is soft, he can play with it with his fingers whenever he likes.

'Have you killed people?' she heard herself ask, again distant from her own voice.

He was silent, it seemed for a long time, looking away, no movement upon his face.

Then he said, 'So have Frank and his brother.'

'No.'

'Oh yes. Off and on over the years, a fair handful.'

'That's a lie.'

'The romance is over Cecily.'

'You're lying.'

He shook his head, sarcasm in his voice. 'Tut tut, Cecily. Cecily, Cecily, they call you Cis don't they? A good upper-class lefty like you, what do you think you are doing with Frank Blake?'

'Maybe it is the kisses. And the fucking,' she said, fiercely, to her distress feeling herself blush red. She wanted to brazen her marriage into his face, against his attempt to defile it. But she couldn't. The onslaught from him was too strong.

'The kissing and the fucking,' he repeated after her, smiling again.

It was horrible. It was intolerable.

'I expect you go around telling yourself that you "love life". Is that what you do?' He paused. 'It's over. You will have to betray him, Cecily. In the end. This is what I have to say to you. In the end, you will have to betray him, understand that. And go back to your own. I mean, what are you going to do? Become his accomplice, his accessory, on a charge of terrorism? And spend twenty-five years in gaol? Do you know what happens to long-term women prisoners? You will get out in the next century.' He bent toward her, leaning on his stick. 'I mean, what will your body be like?'

They stared at each other.

Implacable hatred, thought Cecily, the phrase repeating itself in her head, splintering into meaninglessness. Plac, plac, im, plac plac, tred, tred, tred.

He took a postcard from his pocket. 'Telephone number. It is an answering machine. On a floor in an empty room in London. Utterly safe. Ring day or night. When you want to talk to me, just name the time and the place.' He grinned, at his most boyish. 'The avenger calls.'

And he flicked the postcard. It flutterd to the sand beside her thigh.

'Time and place,' he said again and walked away, hobbling across the uneven sand, seeming to lean against the light, slightly jerky in his movements, as if he were out of synchronisation, askew to the reality of the time and place of the holiday scene around him. She watched him disappear amongst the dark shade of olive trees at the top of the beach.

Feel. Feel anything.

But she felt nothing, the frightening encounter had cut her off from her senses, the sand was neither hot nor cold,

163

the air about her was an inert wall against her skin, her tongue was dead. She unscrewed the bottle of metaxa and tipped it, drinking three gulps.

Flat liquid. Lukewarm, Tasteless. And . . . The brandy flared alive in her throat, a downward flame towards her stomach. She heard children yelling. A family had come onto the beach. Her skin was prickling. Heatwave. The sand was burning. Chatter chatter, a little voice, the owner of the monkey, an arrogant beach boy who clearly worked on his shoulder muscles was lifting the little creature back into the tree. The siesta was over.

Frank, Brian and Elsa came out of the water, gleaming, laughing, pushing each other.

'Brian caught a fucking fish!' cried Frank.

'A fucking fish!' shouted Brian. 'Look!' and held up his fist. In it, a fish. The fish wriggled.

'Poor little fish,' said Elsa. 'It swims, then come the mad English.'

'Put it down her knickers!' said Frank, grabbing Elsa's arm.

'I'll put it down her knickers!' said Brian, alight with the idea.

'You are rude! Poor fish.'

'Lucky fish,' said Frank.

''Ere!' said Brian. 'Lucky fish, eh? Eh? Hold her Frank.'

'Give us a hand here Cis!'

Cicely did not move. They pranced around her yelling, Frank swinging Elsa around.

Brian suddenly screeched and jumped in the air.

'Arrgh! It bloody bit me! This fish bit me!'

Frank was standing still. 'What is it Cis?' Cecily gave a little shake of her head.

'This dago fish bit my hand!' yelled Brian, shaking the fish in his hand vigorously.

Frank turned on him. 'Throw it back in the sea, for fucksake.'

'I'll throw it back in the sea. Come on fish.' And Brian stumbled down the beach purposefully.

'Brian to catch a fish!' laughed Elsa, happily. 'Is there drink?' And she lifted the brandy bottle to her lips.

Frank sat beside Cecily in the sand. 'Who was that geezer?'

Cecily sat still.

'On the raft, I saw you talking to some face.'

'No one.'

'He bother you?'

'It was no one.'

'I mean, here we are on a holiday beach, with families about, and you get kinks bothering you.'

She couldn't bear it. Frank in his public good citizen mode. Tied up an old woman. Glass in her eye. Getting righteous, phoney. You phoney. You liar, you . . .

'I'll send Brian after him for a word.'

'No don't!' She was too sharp. He started and looked at her. 'It doesn't matter, Frank.'

'Say the word, love. Brian will sort him out.'

'No.'

Frank looked down. 'Writing a postcard?'

Peter Carter's postcard still lay by her knee, the picture face up. Blue sky. Greek columns. She felt a thump of panic in her chest.

'Souvenir,' she said, picking up the card. She slipped it into her beach bag.

Frank grunted.

'Brian!' exclaimed Elsa. 'That great lump of English-

man, what does he do in the sea? I do not know what he
does.'

'Go and have a look then,' said Frank, gutterally.

She was trying to read everything in his voice, each
tone, trying to hear it as ugly and dangerous. She wanted
to see him anew, to test what Peter Carter had said and
confirm it. But he was the same. It was just him.

Elsa put the bottle of brandy down and ran toward the
water's edge. 'Brian!' she called, 'you swim with me.'

'Was that kink really bothering you?'

'No.'

Frank sulked. Tell him, Cecily said to herself. Show
him the postcard. Take it out of the beach bag and show
it to him. Ask him what the hell it means, what this Peter
wants.

'Do you like it here?'

'It's lovely . . .', she said.

But how do you ask, in heaven's name, ask the man
you are married to, the lover who is in you, the imprint of
whose hand lies on your inner thigh, whose smell has
seeped into your pores, whose skin is grafted on to you in
patches along your body, how do you ask him if he has
beaten up . . . If he . . . Those things, if . . .

And he was being so like Frank, leaning towards her,
arching his long back to speak to her, intimate and
tender. 'We'll pack up and push off if you don't.'

'Is that what you want to do?' she managed to say.

'No, what d'you want to do, doll?'

'No, Frank. Do you want to leave?'

He shrugged. 'Evens,' he said, lying back, lifting sand,
letting it run between his fingers.

Show him the card, show it to him. She did not.

'Is there a reason why you want to leave? We only just
got here,' she said.

'You tell me,' he said. He snatched at the metaxa bottle and drank.

What was this, jealousy? Because he'd seen her and Carter on the beach? They were in the endgame of a married argument. Just show him the card . . .

And he turned, holding her jaw gently in his hand and kissed her, the taste of his mouth sweet and sour with the brandy and the sea.

'Days of champagne 'n' oranges. Not done yet, eh my love? Eh?'

Frank, or are you a simulacrum? A phoney, in his place, out of the sea. An image of him, without substance. All appearance.

Elsa ran up to them. 'Your brother, the fish. He has ate it.'

'You what?' said Frank.

'He has ate the fish.'

Brian lumbered forward against the sun. He stood before them, legs wide. ''Ere! That fish!' he triumphed, 'I ate it!'

'Raw fish,' nodded Elsa.

'No fucking fish bites me and gets away with it.' He opened the hand. ''Ere's the head.'

A purple, patchy look came over his face.

'Oh poor man,' said Elsa.

'Oh dear,' said Brian.

'How about that, eh?' said Frank, his voice forcing laughter. 'Eh, Cis? Els'? How about my brother! If I am Robin Hood, he is Friar Tuck. Eh Cis?'

Brian bent forward with the air of a man who had done this many times before, balancing himself like a Sumo wrestler, and began a long, gut-wrenching heave.

Cecily stood, put on her beach wrap, picked up her beach bag and walked away, quickly, past the holiday-makers who had appeared for the late afternoon swimming with their raffia bags, beach toys, parasols drink coolers, all of them watching Brian's display with disgust and giggles. Frank did not move. She walked into the little olive grove at the top of the beach.

Gone funny on me. Silly cow, poor silly cow, thought Frank, watching her go.

What's she doing, where are you going, Cis? Time of time-of-the-month is it? No, just going funny on me. Don't she know, don't you know you fucking silly cow, how bad it is for me, what we've got? How much it is tearing me apart.

Tearing apart. 'Cos I am in danger of not keeping this together, this fucking escapade, this helter-skelter. No, she don't even know she's on it. Don't want her to, either. What keeps this circus together. I've got my pride and you're family now, silly cow, walking off and . . . What do you want me to do?

'She is upsetting, I'll go to her . . .', said Elsa.

'Stay where you are,' said Frank. 'Look after Brian.'

Brian was now fully relieved and sitting on his backside with his legs stuck out straight, what he had brought up piled in an oddly neat little mound between his knees, the chewed fish head discernible within it.

'Fucking hell Brian.'

'Sorry Frank.'

Frank glanced back up the beach to the olive grove. Cecily had disappeared. He felt tiredness across his back, as if his shoulder blades were grating beneath the skin.

'Oi, Brian. That.'

'What?' asked Brian, as innocent as a naughty fucking kid. I'll never get a break from you, will I Brian, ever?

Family man I am and it will do for me, in the end.

'Cover that up.'

'Oh. Yeah,' and like a child building a sand castle Brian began to cover over the contents of his stomach. This was too much for a German family sitting five yards away. The overweight father rose in a rage to protest.

'We are now disgusted,' he said, in a heavy accent.

Frank turned and looked at him, a finger raised. The man was at once silent. He said something in German and his family rose, packing their beach equipment.

Frank stood and ran down the beach. Brian watched him, looking up, big trusting eyes. They all trust me. He waded into the water and dived.

Sweet. Nothing. One end of the baths, Camberwell Green, to the other, holding your breath, turn round, all the way back again under water.

Can't hear a fucking thing when you're under water, that's what's so fucking wonderful about swimming. He opened his eyes. The sand stretched clear beneath him under the glass roof of the surface. Again and again, he stroked with his arms, kicked with his legs, his chest was tight, he bubbled air out in little bursts from between his lips, he wanted to go on and on, not surfacing. But he had to, and, gasping, he dog paddled. He had swum half the distance to the raft. He looked back at the beach. He could see Elsa, looking out for him anxiously. She saw him and jumped and waved, happily. He waved back, turned and made for the raft.

Swim through the lot, he thought. He sat on the edge of the raft, legs dangling in the water, ignoring the teenage swimmers who laughed and fooled about behind him.

Each day a swim, and each day as it comes. What else can you do? Do each day, keep together, be there when you're pissed and had a fantastic meal and it's time for beddybyes. Do I believe that? Nah, no way.

Some copper said to me once, you crims work as fucking hard as straight businessmen. Have the same worries. Overheads, marketing, profit 'n' loss. Why do you bother?

Why indeed.

She's softening you, Frank. You know she is. That's what Brian thinks and all, though he'd not say, out of respect. But she is. She is making you fearful, for her. Fearful for her. I fear for you my love.

Oh sod, sod, sod.

My edge will go, her softening. It's not things tearing apart, it's . . . being smoothed. Thinned out. She'll smooth me out. A bar o' fucking soap in her hands. Lathering me up. Blow me away, bubbles between her fingers.

Lucius Cornelius Sulla, Julius Gaius Caesar, Octavius that mean-minded cunt, my Latin heroes, how am I doing? Francus Blacius, going the way of Antony, washed out, washed up by a woman, eh?

I never let on to Cis, did I, that I loved the fucking Latin. Open University. She was improving me, no way could I let on. I could have been something else, she reckoned. Do-gooder. She still is.

And here I am. A bent scholar! He smiled. Resting in my villa on my island. After operations, out on the edge of the Empire, my generals, out on the edge of the known world with the Irish tribes. And going to pieces. The great men look down on me. *Mea culpa.*

Cis's old father. Maybe the generals were like him. I am just a squaddie, in the legions of hardmen.

Frank laughed, startling a scrawny teenage couple who had sat next to him on the raft's edge.

Sir Stephen Rose. Meeting Daddy. What a nightmare I

thought that was going to be. Got on with him like a house on fire, actually.

Evil-minded old bastard, though. Took me punting. Got his new convict son-in-law a-boating, what, chaps. Wanted me to fall in. Lay back there in this punt thing, his stupid fucking boat, pouring himself bubbly, watching me make with the pole. But I got it in one. It's only balance.

A gentleman and a scholar and a right old cunt. A Roman mind there. Arrogant. Watchful. Not really giving a toss. And a great interrogator, I sorted that at once. The crusty sod, half pissed, did not let go for a second. Little questions all the time. Then a shock remark.

'I hope you satisfy my daughter's cunt requirements.'

That's actually what he said to me. I mean, what are these people?

'Don't worry on that score,' I said.

'No no, a father's duty to ask,' he'd said. Yeah, the mind of a copper, but a dodgy one. He had me marked down, in some way. Yeah, we got on like a house on fire. Getting pissed with him alone after the dinner, in his library, decanter sloshing back 'n' forth, I have the thought, hello, he's bent.

Takes one to know one. Cis is straight as a die, her sister too. But the old man? A bent copper? There was stuff, coming out of him in his cups, about the war. And Palestine. Not that that one would tell you anything he didn't want to, even in drink. But he was waving, yeah, he was sending signals that I could not read. Kept on about had I seen a man injured, ever seen a man lose a leg, or get a bullet in the spine, did I have any idea what it would do to a man's mind. What was all that? Weird.

Then there were the books. That was really weird. He took this key out of his trousers, he was pretty wobbly by then, and unlocked the wall. The books, slid them back. And there was all this porn, some of it big books, leather and Latin, one from the middle ages with black and white drawings, woodcuts of nuns being hanged and fucked, alongside New York wank mags, 'Whip Gazette', 'Anal Monthly', that kind of crap. I did not get the point. I think he was showing me some kind of holy of holies, trying to sell me some kind of view of the world. I did not rate it. There he was, a scholar, Cambridge, a philosopher, drooling over that stuff. He should know fucking better.

Why did I think afterwards, that he knew about Ireland? Ireland he did not mention, once. But when he talked about Palestine, back in the forties, some bomb going off in Jerusalem, I dunno, there was a kind of echo. He was talking about Ireland, backhandedly. And when he was showing me his porn, saying things about human nature, mind and body at war, gobbledegook, he was letting me know something, but what? Devious fucker.

What a crowd around the old man, in that house. Books. Leather armchairs, silver. Candles on candelabras at dinner. And a bloody slaughterhouse, yeah the good life in an abattoir. Cis, the sister, that husband of the sister, that Henry, oh dear oh deary me, I think my manner put him off. All of 'em hung about Sir Stephen like sides of meat, in that lovely house, round the old master butcher.

No love. Sir Stephen bloody Rose, eh? Knelt beneath the bread knife, services to Queen and country. Loveless.

Cis had wanted me to meet him, but while we were there she hardly said a thing. She got dolled up, but her eyes were dead, all the afternoon and evening, like she was someone else.

The couple next to Frank on the raft were lying in an embrace, the water gently running over the raft about their legs. Hey ho, thought Frank. He looked back at the beach and could make out the round stomach of his brother, lain out with Elsa beside him.

Hey ho, though empires rise and fall.

And he slipped off the raft and began to swim back to the shore.

I will buy a necklace Cecily thought, loose in the streets of the resort. Tat, tat, give me tat.

A necklace to mark me, a necklace to chain me.

Festoon me in tat.

She was standing, barefoot, wearing her swimsuit and her wrap, in a street market on a sloping road. A powerful smell. She looked down. Fish, laid out on white tin trays on low boxes at her feet, strange fish with red and violet scales and tendrils at their throats, mouths gaping. An old woman smiled and flipped a fish up at her.

'Buy, buy?'

Yes, buy the fish. Hang it round my neck. Go back to the villa, the thing dangling down me. Brian can chew it. Brian can slobber over me, chewing, right Frank? You want that, that a laugh?

But the fish in the old woman's hand moved its mouth. Still alive. Horror. She backed away. The crowd pushed her.

Tat, tat.

At a stall she bought a flimsy pair of gold high-heeled shoes. That's it, tat! Under the shade of the awning two old men on chairs, braces, bellies pushing at collarless shirts, watched her with grins.

Foreign tart. I will festoon me. She slipped the shoes on before the old men's gaze, and paid. Her bag was full of the foreign banknotes given her by Frank. 'Here you are Cis, damage that.' Funny money, pretend money, for the

173

old lechers. She turned with what she hoped was a tarty haughtiness and walked away on the high heels, feeling the muscles of her calves strain, pushing through the market shoppers, tears on her face.

I have dabbled. With the scum. Hard core. Hard water. Pumice stone. Rub the smell of fish from me. Rub, rub.

She stood on a little bridge over the entrance to a lagoon, at the heart of the town. In the brochure Frank had shown her, 'Suck this and see', it had looked so pretty, almost Chinese. It was meant to be bottomless, an entrance to the underworld. Some goddess had swum down, after a lover? It was in all the tourist bumph.

'Magic, magic, it will be magic, Crete.' Here was the reality. Package tourists wandered over the bridge in couples, a shuffling stroll in the press of numbers. The light was going, but she could still see the scruffy edge of the lagoon, walls, the town above, tired trees, litter amongst the sand, teenage English lads sitting desolated by the drinking daylong in the sun.

Shuffle, shuffle, sandals, flip-flops, cheap high heels like hers. Wearing out the magic, wearing out the earth.

A tiny gold handbag hung outside a shop, gold sequins splintering light over her head. Tat, buy that. She did. She slipped Peter Carter's card into it. 'Betray, in the end, you will have to.' In the cramped shop, beneath the counter's glass, there was a tray of necklaces, amongst them a tiny gold double axe upon a chain. Buy that. She did.

She went for a drink at a restaurant bar.

'You will have to betray him, in the end,' said Peter Carter, suddenly, within her inner ear.

She walked through the evening crowds into another bar, drank, then into another. Her stomach began to fill with the warmth of metaxas. She curved her way through the town beneath holiday fairy lights that turned faces to garish masks.

'Don't hurt us, please don't hurt us,' she had said. Implacable hatred, plac, plac, im, plac, plac, tred, tred, tred. Splinter, world. Colours from the fairy lights swirled, like oil, on the surface of the sea.

'Just whom do you think you have married?' the man in black had said.

Peter Carter. A man in black. She had read somewhere about the blackness of comets. Rock so dark it absorbed all the light, returning nothing to the eye. Blacker than black.

I'm so far from home. Oh for a nice cup of tea. Oh for the English weather forecast on the radio, in the kitchen, while stirring a packet of soup, cooking some cheese on toast.

Go back to my own. Be on the lawn for Daddy, with Matty, safe. 'The romance is over,' said the Devil. When he came up to me on the beach. To collect my soul.

I am getting very drunk.

She was in a bar at the edge of the town, by the water. It wasn't frequented by tourists. There were round tables with pillars rising through them, you sat on stools. The walls were of pale green plastic tiles. A hatch-door in her drunkenness opened. She saw the place she had ended up in. She was the only woman there. She sensed that her presence was, in some way, unpardonable. This was a functional drinking hole, away from the illusion of the resort, the colour, the shops, the cafés and restaurants. This was the engine room of the tourist funfair the town had become. Here the boiler stokers sat, silent and hunched, clicking dominoes, flicking dog-eared cards on the small tables.

The sadness of drunken philosophical thoughts washed

175

through her. She remembered the sadness one night with Frank, in the West End, when they left some club of black dresses and heavy scent, and they saw, from the window of a minicab, the girls who worked the club's clients going home. In the club they had seemed fabulous, in the ultra-violet light filtered through smoke haze, the porcelain skin of their bare arms and shoulders shining against their tight black dresses. Now, going home at four in the morning, the magnificent creatures who had inflamed the fantasies of middle-aged businessmen to the tune of seventy-five pounds for a bottle of inferior champagne, could have been a group of cleaners, from a late-night office job, their hairdos a mess, their crumpled leather coats and anoraks bundled about them, old jeans, their high heels the only sign of their dreary profession. They were very young, and tiny, they looked tired out.

Fantasy's working class.

That's who these men are, philosophised Cecily. The working class of our magic break in the sun, the boiler stokers from the hold of the fancy tourist ship, the town that sailed on the night of shish kebabs and Greek dancing bands. Our funny holiday-makers' money becomes their crumpled, dirty banknotes, laid in bets on their card games. This is the scruffy kitchen in the fairground, round the back from the ghost train, the hall of mirrors and the Dutch organ, where the fairground hands drink their foul-smelling tea and slugs of white liquor from the chipped glasses held in their fists.

Go. I'll go. I've got the Visa card, I've got drachmas, a hundred English pounds, fine, but Frank's got my ticket. He keeps the tickets. Funny about that, he'd look at them all the time as if air tickets were dangerous, their ink not to be trusted, but that's all right, the Visa card will get me a flight. A taxi to Heraklion Airport. Out, out I'll get out.

Tomorrow morning, I'll be listening to Radio Four, the weather, making toast. Flight, to English toast and English weather, to what I know.

Oh God.

Frank's got my passport. He's got all our passports. He's even funnier about passports than airline tickets. I've seen him, sitting there, staring at them, at the photographs, running his finger over them, lost in thought.

No, he's not got Elsa's passport. I saw her say no, with a little shake of her head. She wouldn't give it to him. There is a woman of the world, with her escape. I have been conned, I have been . . .

A man slipped onto the stool beside her. 'Come here often, do you?' he said. It was Frank. 'You silly cow, you poor silly cow,' he said, as she hid her face against his shoulder. 'You are pissed as a newt my love. How did you find this place?'

'Don't know. Ended up here.'

'Not a good place, this Cis.'

'Why? Do you know it?'

'Brian checked it out.'

Am I now to be afraid of you, Frank?

'Here!' He laughed. 'I followed you all over town. You left a great impression in a lot of bars.'

'Did I?'

'Blazed a trail my love. Men on the floor with their legs in the air everywhere I went. Hey Marcos.' A big man at the bar with a grizzled beard and a dirty towel in his hands turned to Frank. 'Get us a taxi. Taxi?'

'You . . .', she felt her mouth slurring . . . 'know them here?'

'I told you, Brian checked the place out.'

Of course he knows them, he would know everyone in a place like this, anywhere in the world. These are his people, these are his fish in the sea. Fish. Gills moving on a white metal tray. She swallowed against a rush of nausea.

'Life is a doddle, is it Frank?' she said.

'Too right. Leave it to me.'

The coffee was full of grounds. She sat naked on the edge of the bed of the big bedroom in the villa, her feet cold on the tiles, looking out into the dark beyond the balcony, the sea and the outline of an island dim beneath the starlight. The drink made her feel feverish, the cold of the tiles was delicious on the soles of her feet. On an impulse she lay down on the floor and pressed her cheek against the tiles. Their cold ran the length of her body. She reached for the coffee and knocked the mug over. No handle, it rolled. She shivered, Oh I am going to be really ill. She drew her knees up to her chest, feeling small. It was the big-little sensation she had shared with Matty, she had it badly. The room expanded, the bed was huge above her, its edge ten, twenty feet high, the ceiling a vault, way above, the tiles a hard plain stretching for miles to the balcony, squared, geometric barren fields glowing faintly by starlight.

'Doll?'

Doll, am I. Frank leant over her. Keep still.

'You knocked your coffee over,' he said, as if puzzled.

'It . . .' Her throat was sticky. 'It had grounds.'

'Yeah. Real coffee, in't it.'

The room collapsed back to its normal size. He had simply poured water over coffee ground, as if it was Nescafé, she realised. Domestic he was not. What would he make of scrambled eggs?

He crouched by her, showing a gentle concern, his

voice velvety, she could not tell whether with real feeling or utterly phoney. I am in such trouble, she thought. My faith, it's shot to pieces, my faith in him.

'Hey,' and now he knelt to pick her up.

'No . . .', she said, putting out a hand to ward him off, but with no force.

'Here we go,' and he lifted her. She was light, no strength, her joints loose and watery, her bones as if of plasticine, bendy. She could be moulded, she could be rolled up and squeezed into a child's tin box, old plasticine, all the colours run together. Frank lay her on the quilt of the bed and flipped it over her, patting it softly around her form. Then he lay beside her, the quilt between them. He stroked her hair. He was irritating her, even the slight pull of her hair on her scalp was too much. She didn't close her eyes, she didn't look at him, she kept utterly still. He stopped stroking her hair.

'You had a skinful,' he said.

He put his hand beneath her neck, to lift her head. She grimaced. He withdrew his hand.

'I'll make you some more coffee.'

'Frank. You don't just pour the water onto real coffee,' she said from the depth of the quilt, sleepily, closing her eyes now.

'No?'

'No.'

He paused. 'What do you do then?'

She was very nearly asleep, lying before the first state of dreaming where irrationality begins to slant things, this time making the quilt build around her into banks of soft warm cloud, that, somehow, had a windmill within it, with a white sail, turning silently. She could feel herself smiling. 'You . . .', she said, her voice faint, 'percolate'.

'Ah, right,' he said and slipped away.

She moved towards the first dream, into the mist of the clouds which sped past her, she was nearing the white-sailed windmill. The sails began to change shape as they turned, becoming huge double-edge axes. There was menace here. She was flying through the air toward one of the sails, which was huge, it billowed, there were tears and stains within its cloth. She was growing longer, stretching, her back arched to the shape of the axe blade, and she realised that Frank had come back to the bed, naked, beneath the quilt and was straddling her, holding her up to him with his arms around the small of her back.

'Frank, no . . .'

'Cis, give me this one, I wanted to, when you were asleep,' he could hardly talk. His breath was stale, unusually for him he had not showered and shaved before coming to bed, he was goaty with the day's sweat, the salt of the afternoon's swimming.

'Oh Frank.' She lifted herself up, locking her ankles together behind his back, with a desperate surge of strength she swept the pillows away and threw her head back. She felt so light, like a girl, her legs were so thin, the muscles a helpless jelly hanging in her skin. She pushed her palms against the wall. The bed skidded out into the room on its castors across the tiles. Frank started. He was about to protest, or laugh, or draw back.

'No, go on, go on,' she managed to say. His mouth came down on her throat, his bristles scraping her skin. She reached up and clung at his shoulder blades with her nails as he sank himself into her. The tower of the windmill, she remembered, just as he had woken her, she was stopping it turning into the dark man as you can at a certain moment stop dreams becoming nightmares, saying, no the tower will not be Peter Carter in black with his stick, which he whirls, round and round. No! And her strength was back, she fought, she was trying to turn him, she tore at his back, she forced herself up trying to grip him with the muscles within her. And they were equals again, as she always made them in their lovemaking, at her insistence, for she had always sworn to herself that neither of them would ever distinguish between the taker and the taken.

She woke. Light was everywhere in the room. The bed was in the centre, skewed at an angle to the walls. The quilt was on the floor, the sheet was half off, revealing the mattress beneath. She sprawled, she turned, trying to drag the sheet around her. She gave up.

I have a tin-opener stuck in my head, she thought. I'll mow the lawn.

And came to. She wasn't in the cottage in Kent. Where then? Daddy's house. The flat. No.

And she experienced that rearrangement when you wake of what has happened and where you are, the shaking of a kaleidoscope to return the coloured fragments to a picture. Shake, ah yes. That is who I am, this is where I am and this is what is happening to me. She closed her eyes.

Already the air had the metallic taste of a hot Mediterranean day.

She realised she had seen him. He was out on the balcony, crouched down, his back to the sea. She opened her eyes.

'Frank?'

The little trashy gold bag she had bought the previous night was by his feet. He was staring at Peter Carter's postcard.

181

She felt nothing. I can shout at him for looking in my bag. I can be scared. I can lie, there's just a phone number, a London phone number on it. A friend of Matty's. Call her . . . Abigail. Yes, Abigail, ring her when I get home, old girlfriend. Knew her at school. Oh, oh, oh.

'He gave it to me,' she heard herself say, the shock that she was going to tell him the truth heavy at the back of her mouth.

Frank did not look up. He was picking at the corner of the postcard, as if trying to peel the picture from it, it was the way he looked at airline tickets and passports, with slow, rapt concentration. Like a gorilla, she thought, in a zoo, picking up a cigarette packet thrown into the cage by a spectator. The great animal turning it, gravely, before his deep, sad eyes.

'The man on the beach. He said his name was Peter Carter.'

What is in a name? Frank made no movement.

'Remember,' she tried again. 'That man, you asked me if he was bothering me . . .'

'Yeah, yeah,' said Frank, dully.

She had thought he would stride to the bed in a rage, hit her for the first time in their life, scream and shout. But he stayed on the balcony, crouched, seeming to cower from the light at his back.

'Frank, he said . . .'. she sat up, pulling the blanket about her. 'Do you want me to tell you what he said?'

'Said he wanted you to ring this number, didn't he? Any time you want to grass me.'

She paused. 'How did you know?'

'I rang it. An hour ago.'

She couldn't read him, she couldn't tell his mood. 'What . . .'

'Fucking answering machine. A geezer's voice said your name.'

'Said my name?'

' "Speak after the tone, Cecily." That's all.' He paused, then said, in a dull voice, still looking down, 'Have you? Spoken after the tone?'

'No. No.'

A silence. And she was angry, I'll hit you in the face, if you will not hit me, she thought. I'll beat it out of you, what this danger is. It is dangerous, I know, I can feel it between us.

'Frank, talk to me, tell me why this man is after you.'

'I thought he was dead, that's all,' he said and shrugged.

The gesture appalled her, his weariness, his casualness. Dead, not dead, a shrug. She knew she was looking into the abyss of the man's life, this stranger, and she could see nothing.

'Days of champagne 'n' oranges. Not done yet,' said Frank, but sadly, quietly, in a manner quite unlike him.

'No?'

He looked at her, his lips parted, making some kind of judgement. He seemed so low.

Then he was up on his feet. At a suitcase. Her passport was thrown towards her on the bed. 'Out of this dump, now, we go . . .', he was saying. 'Brian! Brian! Els'!' he was shouting.

'Frank . . .'

He came to her and held her head in his hands. 'Don't worry 'bout that guy, he is a loner, a loser. No one gets to us, eh my love? Fire, water . . .' Shouting again. 'Brian for fucksake!' And back to her, his hands gentle and warm beneath her jaw. He kissed her full on her mouth. 'Absolutely no one, my love. I mean I am Robin Hood.'

183

'Robbing Irish post offices?' she said.

He looked at her, it seemed for a long time, with nothing in his eyes.

Then he said, 'I want you to go with Elsa.'

'What? . . .'

'We'll get new tickets. At the airport. You'll go to Cologne with her. Then on by train, to Amsterdam.'

'Frank, no, we can't split up . . .'

'She's got a nice place there, quiet, out of the way. Be just a few days. You get on with Els' don't you? Kraut trains are great. Waiters in the buffet, bring you your drinkies.' He took his hands from her head and held up the postcard. 'You want this?' he said, softly.

'No.' She shook her head, unable to say more.

'You're free, y'know,' he said. 'You are. I want you to know that.'

'We're married, Frank.'

'Freely. A modern couple of the world, my love. Look after this.'

And he flicked the postcard to her. She looked at it, it seemed for a very long time.

She didn't understand, did he expect her to telephone Carter's answering machine and betray him, after all? Did he want that?

She pushed the card away from the bed, onto the floor. 'No.' she said.

'Good girl,' he said, so softly it was almost a whisper, and kissed her, formally, upon the forehead. Then he was striding about the room, shouting, flinging suitcases on the bed beside her, as if she were not there, still naked, the sheet half draped about her. 'Brian? Where the fuck are you? We're getting the fuck out of here.'

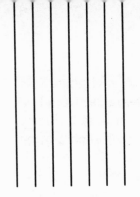

Matty watched television every afternoon. It was a vice she tried to hide, for she told herself it was a vice. Though whom she was hiding this simple pleasure from she didn't know, there was no one to disapprove, or care less. Not Henry, not the latest maid, a Malayan girl whom they called Flower, the third since the Liverpudlian maid Tracey had disappeared taking with her Matty's credit cards and, as far as they could tell, twelve silver forks. But, incomprehensibly, no knives to match. Henry had raved but Matty just cancelled the cards and shrugged the incident off. Another mysterious soul that girl, wandering the earth towards a bad end. Like Cis.

Matty followed the obscurer Australian soap operas, the tangled story lines of love and car crashes, glumly acted out on studio verandas. She practised the vice with a portable television set high in her father's house, in an attic bedroom, which had been Cecily's when they were girls.

The last time she had seen her sister was the occasion when she had brought Frank to meet their father. And what an occasion. Henry had been half scared to death. Frank had looked wonderful, big, beautifully dressed, 'spivvy', Henry had called him. And indeed Frank had looked outrageous, like a successful boxer, in a silk tie and dark grey suit, in which he effortlessly punted their father out on the river. Henry had not known what to do. And Daddy had lavished attention on the guest, closeting him-

185

self away with him after dinner. Henry's nightmare was that the will would be redrawn, and the house would go to this rival, this glamorous second son-in-law. Matty knew her father was quite capable of doing such a thing but did not care less. It was not that she had become reconciled to Sir Stephen's machinations, or felt any sense of devil-may-care revolt. Her state was sadder, for Matty had become worn out. She had let go and she knew it.

She had known it on the afternoon that Cecily had brought Frank to the house, a different Cecily, 'looking like a tart', the frazzled Henry had sneered. They had tried to talk, on the lawn, as they had so often. But her sister seemed to be dreaming, in a hard shell. She wore a sharp scent, something she would never have done before. 'Smelt like a tart too.' Oh shut up, Henry. A hard shiny shell within which she shone, looking very beautiful, and calm. She knew they were living in the cottage, but they had changed the telephone number. When she asked why, Cecily would not say, nor, so hurtfully, did she offer the new one. The complicity between them seemed never to have existed. 'Is it all right? Are you all right? Married life? . . .', she had tried to ask. But all Cecily would say was, 'Yes,' almost haughtily, unsmiling. An alarming phrase had come to Matty, 'Playing a queen of crime'. Playing a queen of crime. She was helpless before the performance. When they had left, Cecily driving a flushed, relaxed Frank who had hugged her on the steps of the house, Matty had come up here, to this room, to cry. But no tears had come. She had sat in the dark, feeling her sister had gone for ever, and that the contest between them was, after so many years, over.

Now the little room was full of light from a large dormer window. Its wallpaper of friendly cartoon parrots oddly interspersed with posies of English flowers, daffodils and primroses, nursery wallpaper, was faded now and in one corner, to the outside wall of the house, there was a brown stain. But the room retained its freshness. It was a haven, a tree-house for secrets, high above her father's domain in the rooms and the garden below. She needed it all the more now that her father had gone so strange, so difficult.

On the screen the flying doctor's wife had just learnt, from the eternally malicious female neighbour, that her husband was flying regularly to the arms of an outback farmer's daughter. All this programme lacks is fuck scenes, she thought to herself, reaching for a chocolate. Chocolate eating was part of the vice, with Martini and lemonade. She should have ice cubes with the Martini, but that would mean stealing them from the kitchen. Which was her own kitchen, but she did not want to be found out. She kept the Martini and lemonade bottles beneath the single bed. Yes, some good fuck scenes. But no. The fucking goes on during the commercial breaks. As in real life. As with Rodney. While eyes are turned away from the screen, as some tyre or beer advert is distracting the nation and no one is watching, we rut.

Though in fact she had not been to London for three months, under cover of 'shopping', to the little house hidden at the back of Waterloo. They had not broken with each other, the affair had just fallen into dereliction. Always she had called him, at a number that rang in the little house, to confirm the next time. She just hadn't rung. As the weeks went by and he made no attempt to reach her, she put on weight, she thickened, chocolates and television in the afternoons ... I balloon, she thought, wanting to hate herself, feeling she really should hate herself. But self-loathing was too great an effort. Daddy often calls himself a ritualist, I am caught in a ritual. I am so tired in the afternoons, I don't know why, what do I do in the mornings? By the afternoon it is difficult to remember. I balloon, a heavy old balloon left over from Christmas, not lead, but chocolate. Chocolate balloon. But I need comfort, I need a rest in the afternoons, I need a sprawl. Upon the television screen, to slow and sinister music, the flying doctor's wife was sliding open a drawer, in the drawer there were old love letters. From Rusty, her last affair but two, wasn't it? Rusty was 'an engineer' from Sydney, half her age and with loins like callipers, tightly bejeaned. Now she was standing, letters in hand, beside a telephone and the music was soaring. The telephone had a little quilt upon the handle of the receiver, like a tea cosy. What a weird country Australia must be. The young men seem to have great crotches though. The flying doctor's wife lifted the telephone. So Rusty's coming back into the programme. Good. But I suppose that awful mother of his will tag along too, to get some moralising in.

Into adverts again. That's that for this afternoon. She turned the television set off. She ran her fingers over the chocolate box. The crinkly brown paper crackled, it seemed loudly, in the silence of the little room. Outside it was an autumn afternoon, with the light going. The last of weak ochre sunlight shafted into the room. Motes of dust hung in the air. Was it in the single bed in the corner, now stripped of sheets, covered by a candlewick bedspread, that she and Cis had giggled, late into the nights, under the bedclothes when they were children? There seemed no memories here, none at all. It was just a small room, quite dead.

She went to the window and looked down. Henry was walking with another man. Henry was home, what day was it, oh yes Friday, he'd come back from town early.

He'd taken to doing that. Now that Daddy's not the power he was anymore, you are on the slide, aren't you, husband? He had not been up to find her in the house. Who was he with? Some second-rate crony he'd brought back, to impress with Daddy's house. Well, he's not going to sleep up here. She closed the box of chocolates and screwed on the tops of the Martini and lemonade bottles. Empties rolled against the wainscot and chinked. Oh God, I should clean it out under here, she thought, I must get round to that. Most of the boxes underneath the bed were empty. Amassed guilt. And she stopped still with a sudden realisation. She went quickly to the window.

Henry was on the lawn with Rodney.

In a fury she ran down into the house. She caught sight of herself in a mirror on the lower landing. Oh God. And her face was red and blushing. She went back into a bathroom. Lipstick, do her face. She began to make up, but then the fury hit her again. She'd drunk more Martini than she liked to think. Sod it! What is he doing here, how dare he? She found herself slashing at the mirror with the lipstick then throwing it into the hand basin. It bounced with a ping, flew over her shoulder and rattled in the bath. Sod sod sod! She ran down into the living room and out onto the lawn.

Henry turned to her and introduced her lover to her. They shook hands, like clockwork dolls, like machines.

My husband has introduced my lover to me. How do they do this in the Australian soaps? We should all be sort of making glances at each other and loving it. But it's horrible.

He looks strained. He is thinking I look fat.

'Rodney's come to see Father,' said Henry.

Why does he call my father his father, now? How long has he been doing that?

'Has he been out today?' asked Henry.

Matty stood rooted to the spot, dumb.

'Darling, has Father been out in the air already?'

She shook her head.

'I'll go and get him. Last of a nice day and he'll need his air, if he's not had it,' and Henry walked to the house.

Rooted, dumb with shame. Rodney was seeing the ritual of Sir Stephen, now much incapacitated, taking his time on the lawn for the day. She did not want him to see how inane routines had come to dominate their lives in the house. How dotty they were becoming, prematurely dotty.

'I did my best not to come to your home,' Rodney said.

'What a glaringly stupid remark,' she said. What was extraordinary was that she knew, the moment he opened his mouth, that it was all over between them. Just like that.

'I don't want any embarrassment,' he continued. 'But I have to see your father. Couldn't you just . . . go out?'

Just like that. And he was compounding it. He was so inept, so second-rate. She laughed in his face.

He spoke again. 'The last thing I want to do is come between you and Henry.'

'Oh I don't know,' she said. 'It'll be quite interesting, the two of you together. I think they call it a Bangkok sandwich.'

He looked at her, watery eyed. 'What?'

'No, that's two women and a man together.'

'Have you been drinking?'

She clapped her hands. 'Getting fat, too? See?' She half turned her behind toward him.

'Matty, for Godsake.'

Then she had an inspiration. 'Where is my sister?' she

asked. From the look on Rodney's face, she knew she was right. He's here about Cis.

'Please', said Rodney, 'behave. I beg you.'

Behave? Wait a moment, she thought, feeling excited. Do I have a choice? Can I behave badly then? Yes, of course I bloody well can.

From the house Henry was leading Sir Stephen, who was hung about with rugs and scarves. Sir Stephen was waving and prodding a walking stick into the turf. Bizarrely, in the other hand he held an unopened pint bottle of milk. Henry, one hand under the old man's arm, carried a wicker bucket-chair with the other. A procession of two, thought Matty, a grotesque procession. I am coming alive again, she thought. For the first time in ages I can look at them.

Rodney stepped back from her. Clearly shocked at the sight coming towards them, he said, 'Your father looks . . .'

'Oh yes,' she said. 'Very much so.'

Henry planted the chair, testing for wobble. Henry, do give it a rest, she thought, do you still think you will get the house, even now, pretending to be a nanny to him when he is gaga?

Sir Stephen would not sit down.

'Please sit down Father,' said Henry.

'Who is that?' said Sir Stephen, raising his walking stick beneath a tartan blanket.

Rodney could not take his eyes off the bottle of milk that Sir Stephen clutched, held upright.

'It's Rodney Court,' said Henry. 'He asked to come down.'

'Down? Where?'

'Down to see you, Daddy,' Matty intervened, talking

loudly. He's happy, he's in the pink. You can treat him this way, as if he were a child. He's fine.

'And did he?'

'Oh God,' said Rodney.

'Something wrong?'she countered.

'No, I . . .'

'They think it was a stroke,' she said evenly. 'Though when it happened exactly, we don't know. A minor stroke, he's over it. He exploits it, that's all. Be careful.' I've given you one warning, she thought. That's all you're going to get.

'What is the milk?' Rodney said to her.

'The milk is milk,' she said.

'Ah.' He turned to the old man. 'Sir Stephen,' he said, his embarrassment patent, 'how are you going along?'

'Not on wheels,' replied Sir Stephen.

'Yes?'

'No.'

Henry was becoming irritated. 'Here is your chair.'

'You want me to take the chair?'

'Yes,' said Henry, high voiced.

'But has the agenda been rigged?'

'Daddy, let me help you sit down,' said Matty, thinking, I know you are playing them along, I know you are having one of your better days.

'Thank you my dear,' said Sir Stephen and sat, with some pomp, allowing Matty to spread the blankets about his legs.

There was a silence. Go on, Daddy, she thought. See them off.

'Yes,' said Sir Stephen.

Another punishing silence followed. Then he continued.

'Yes, the swans were all marked this year. Two nicks on the beak. The Vintners' company have the right on

this stretch of the river. Vicious bloody birds. But the
swan master got every one of the cunts.'

Matty watched Rodney nodding as if something wise
had been said. Right, she thought.

'Where is my sister?' she said. 'You're here to talk
about what is happening to her. You too, Henry?'

'I . . .', said Henry. Oh you old boys' network. Network, hairnet, a stocking over a criminal face. The three
men before her were all masked, she knew it.

She turned on Sir Stephen. 'What do you know, father?
You senile, sick old man, have you been playing with
your daughter's life?'

Great! she thought. Keep at it, Matty girl, before they
run the adverts, projected from outer space, over the
lawn, over the back of the ugly house behind us.

'The swan master,' said Sir Stephen. 'Ha! If he misses
a bird, it is the personal property of the Queen. How
magnificently obtuse this country can be.'

'Listen to me! Pay attention to me!' she shouted.

'Matty,' Henry said, 'you are becoming hysterical.'

'What?' she spat into his face. 'You what?'

And Henry was being pompous, pomping, you are
pomping, husband. Pumping out sentences. 'There is something very serious concerning this family. More dangerous than you can know. Rodney here is Junior Minister
for the Army, and you should not know this, I suppose,'
this with a little laugh, he is thinking he is the tops, really
there, 'Rodney is responsible for, well, some highly sensitive security matters.'

'Henry, please,' said Rodney, in a state of terror.

For a second she thought, shall I do this? Or shall I
walk away, round to the kitchen, and make us all tea, and
let these three, this gawky ill-fitted trio of men get on
with it?

Hell no.

And she heard herself saying, 'Oh wow. "Matters!"
What, that my sister's husband robs banks in Ireland? That
he was recruited by Rodney here, and paid for information about the Provisional I.R.A.? And is a kind of criminal
cum, what, agent provocateur? Is he playing the Irish off
against the British, is that what the stupid, beautiful
hunk my sister loves is trying to do? And that my sister's
life is in terrible risk? Where is she? Being hunted, right
now, by Irishmen, by your people, Rodney? Are those the
"Matters"? The "Matters" that matter?'

She looked at Henry. He smiled. The smile of a silly
ass. She looked at Rodney. He closed his eyes. She looked
at her father. He was rocking in his chair, side to side,
with rage.

'How did this . . . woman,' he managed to say, 'This
. . . girl . . . learn of matters of state?'

'This girl is your daughter,' she said, with a mad
impulse to curtsey to him and sit at his feet, her legs
tucked under her, content.

'Daughters?' Said Sir Stephen. 'What daughters?'

You old bastard, she thought.

Henry was pomping again. 'Matty you are being more
foolish than you can realise. You have no idea of what is
at stake.'

'At stake? You want to know what's at stake?'

'Matty,' said Rodney, 'we want cool heads here, and
hearts . . .'

She turned to Henry and said, evenly, as simply as she
could, 'I introduced Cis's roaring boy, gaolbird husband
to the Junior Army Minister here. In the Junior Army
Minister's little London house. His little *pied-à-terre*.'

'Oh no,' said Rodney, under his breath.

'Where I go. When I go down to town. Every Thursday afternoon. To sleep with him.'

To her amazement Henry seemed to consider this quite calmly. 'But you go down to Harrods on Thursdays. Or you did, until recently. The Food Hall. For good cheese. At Harrods.'

'Look old man . . .', began Rodney.

'What is it?' demanded Sir Stephen. 'What are you all talking about now?'

Matty leaned over her father, as if to be kind. 'Listen carefully, Daddy. I've been unfaithful to my husband.' She pointed at Henry. 'Him. By sleeping with . . .', she pointed at Rodney, 'him. Clear now, father?'

'Really?' said Sir Stephen, at the most alert he had been during the confrontation. 'Which one's best at it?'

'You, my wife . . .', said Henry.

'Old man this is nothing,' said Rodney.

'Both pretty weedy actually, Father.'

Henry took two steps towards Rodney.

Rodney took two steps back. 'Henry, I am here to help your family. Your sister-in-law could be involved in the greatest scandal, to do you no end of harm . . .'

'Harm? You talk to me of harm?'

'For Godsake man, there is a war in Ireland. In matters of security what does a quick poke on the side matter?' Rodney turned to Matty. He took her arm. From Henry there was a howling noise. 'Peter Carter. You remember?'

'Yes,' she said.

'He was shot. Nearly died.'

'Because of Frank?' she said.

The little conversation was the last between them, in front of old Sir Stephen in his chair and her husband, who howled on, now sunk on his knees. They spoke

195

evenly, as if they were alone, casually, off-hand.

'My head's on the block for this, Matty. We've lost control of Carter. He's pursuing them. On his own. Your father knew him once, I came for advice. But . . . I don't know what I can do, Matty.'

'Pursuing?'

'There are wild men, both sides of the divide.'

'Where is my sister?' He knew. It is just a game to them, she thought. It is a script conference, isn't that how they make the soaps? They sit around and say, 'Hey, bring Rusty back', 'Hey, lose the husband's legs in a plane crash'. And there it is, for people like me, on the screen to cry over and eat chocolates. They were meeting to decide what to do with my sister's life. To have her taken to Ireland? To rescue her, helicopters, guns blazing? To abandon her? Then they would have gone into Daddy's library, made the phone calls, and drunk whisky. Another episode done. It's not real to them. She hit Rodney full in the face, with her fist clenched. He made a little noise, raising both his hands to his cheek.

'We had a report . . . She was in Cologne.' He couldn't speak. He took his hands from his face. A bulge had appeared on his jaw. 'She got on a train. To Amsterdam. Don't know more.'

And Henry rose from his knees, still howling.

'I think I . . . must let your husband throw me in the river now . . .', Rodney said, trying to smile as Henry crashed into him. They ran across the lawn, Henry pulling at Rodney's clothing, Rodney trying to slap him away.

Matty turned to her father, who sat inert, hunched in the blankets. 'I don't forgive you,' she said.

'For what?' he said.

There were shouts from the river bank. Sir Stephen began to struggle, trying to stand.

'Bloody fools!' he said. 'Disturb the swans! Can knock a man to the ground! Can kill a man!'

He had got to his feet. He still held the milk bottle dead upright before him.

To Matty the scene on the lawn had been shot through with the crass values of a television soap opera. To Sir Stephen it was a ritual, of difficulty and mystery, enacted beneath high vaults. The stroke had left his vision affected, elongating everything. Everyone was unnaturally tall and thin. Heads were long and bulbous and curved away, following the lines of the vaults above. The effort to understand exhausted him. At times there were routines, in the language they were intoning, that he could take part in. When someone mentioned the swans. And sometimes there was a riposte demanded of him, that he thought he could fit into the question and response demanded, but he knew he was faking, he was busking his way through. Fortunately they didn't seem to notice, the ceremony they were involved in had its own text that they knew by heart. The responses he gave seemed to keep his end up.

But what was the ceremony, what the rite? He remembered his name, Rose, could this be the fabled Secret Society of the Rose? Was he an initiate then, only on the edge? Or was he now at the centre, under the vaults his mind made in the sky? And were the dead members of The Rose to be here, Julian the Apostate, Newton, Mozart, Baudelaire, Cocteau, the Divine Marquis himself? The keepers of the secret at the heart of history . . .

Matty was saying something. Sometimes it would clear. Clear sky was there, this fellow Rodney whatsit had come down from London. At these moments, which lasted only a few seconds, Sir Stephen could grasp the obscenity of his predicament. Give me leukaemia, oh Gods, give me rotting flesh, give me blindness, but not a mind blasted to pieces. That is cruel, that is more than the indifference of matter. How can I fight this without memory, without being able to see the ideas hand in hand through an argument, how can I struggle against this illness if I cannot even say to myself, 'I am me?' I . . . Then it would all slant away. The terrible thing about the distortion was that it was not just a visual phenomenon. Thought itself elongated and bent, curved and crisscrossed into vaults. Time jumped. Lines of thought broke, then jumbled, like yarrow sticks thrown at random. Yes. Like . . . What? One image did not refer to another, metaphor was impossible. Suddenly he was accused by one of the celebrants of having daughters. Calumny. He denied it. Now his daughter was striking a man. Now she was turning to forgive him. Forgive him what? Now the ceremony was disintegrating, two men were running across the lawn, shouting. Their invocations had failed. Out on the water they were murdering swans. Why am I holding a bottle of milk?

. . . Of human kindness, he thought, later that night sitting in his library, after there had been shouting and banging of doors in the house, a man coming in, Henry, he left, that is why I was going around all day holding a bloody bottle of milk, out of some train of thought, I knew it was something elaborate. For Godsake! He had a whole crate of milk bottles beside his chair, all unopened. Gold top. He had no memory of demanding them. I must have given them a terrible time, he thought, and smiled, pleased that his sense of malice had also returned. He tilted his head to see the part of the room he wanted, for half of his vision had blacked out. He knew a second stroke was in train, yes in train, a bejewelled train, the cloth shining with precious stones torn out of the side of his head, but thought was back. God the force of it. A lesion in the mind, a great plume shoots out of the side of your head into space and hangs there, frozen gas. That is why I can see only half the room, half of my mind has squirted away.

But the 'I' of me, the persona is back. These few minutes. Time is back, the ideas are still here, I remember the books. Memory is back, there I am, standing in Palestine. My secrets are returned to me. Quick! Quick!

He knew he was weeping. That the first stroke should eradicate everything, for a set of overwhelming and utterly incoherent images which he dimly remembered . . . He had been in a strange cathedral, at a ceremony . . . He had not known his own daughter . . . Now that whatever it was that was destroying him had returned, momentarily restoring him to himself, he realised that no one would ever know what he was thinking, at this moment, no one will ever know. Paper. No time. Leave some kind of mark. Write on the wall. But the walls were full of books . . . Climb to the ceiling, defy gravity at death, to write there . . . Need a step ladder. In the outside scullery. Will never make it.

A ringing had begun in his ears, it was joined by a base note, a low hiss, just out of phase, a fugal harmony. Something is rushing towards me. When it goes minor to major I'll be done for. The well-tempered clarity of death.

I know you don't forgive me, Matty.

He fumbled with his keys. They were in his left-hand pocket, the side his vision was blacked out. He brought his hand to his left side. There they were. He stumbled toward the classical texts, bent over to try to keep the slanted vision upright. The edge of the blacked-out region was shot through with rainbow colours, it was crackling with sparks. No, stars. Here come the stars. The fugue hammered into dissonance in his ears. Leave a sign. Quick! Quick!

He unlocked the wallcase of books, he heaved it open, then with a huge effort he embraced a shelf of the hidden books and pulled them onto the floor.

Matty and Henry were sitting in the kitchen, into the third hour of the row. They were now out of the second reconciliation and into recriminations again. The cocoa she had made was going cold, undrunk, before them. She was exhausted. They were going round and round. How often could they repeat these phrases, how often could they say, 'It's my life'? Tear-stained, slurred by earlier whisky drinking, revived by a brief bout of throwing up, Henry now had a second wind, going through it all again. I did not realise he was so innocent, she thought, still in a kind of childhood, and therefore so easily hurt. In the end we'll have to settle for a nice cup of cocoa and go to sleep, can't he see that?

'Shall I . . . make more cocoa?' she said, wearily. She didn't know if she actually heard a crash from the library, or if it was an instinct, a once in a lifetime transference from father to daughter. She stood up. Her chair fell behind her. Henry stared at her with his mouth open, wrecked, pink-faced.

'What are you doing now?' he said, thickly.

She stood before the scene in the library. Henry blundered into the room behind her, saying something and stopped, silenced. The wall of the room was open. She had never known that could be done. Sir Stephen lay dead before them, face down. Around him there was a pile of books, all open, a great fan of pages. A funeral bier, she was to think, later. In shock, Matty and Henry stooped and looked. Leafed one against another were pages of Latin and Greek, and pornographic images, some magazines, some strange and old. And they were wet, for over them all, drenching them, Sir Stephen had poured bottle after bottle of milk, uniting the pages into a crinkling morass of the sacred and profane.

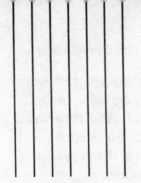

At Heraklion airport, tourists returning home sat in clumps on the floor, or slept against bags and rucksacks in each other's arms, waiting for flights that were hours late. In the morass of people, suntans were beginning to fade, the dreams of beaches and light-filled holidays were dissipating in the airport's squalor. It was in these circumstances that Frank said confused goodbyes to her and to Elsa, a young man and woman in shorts lying eyes closed on a sleeping bag on the airport's floor between them. Frank thrust air tickets into her hand and backed away.

'This is the check-in queue, you'll be O.K., yeah?'

He wasn't going to stay, he wasn't going to see them onto the plane? Was he scared? Were they being watched? Was Carter somewhere here, was that it?

She tried to take his hand. Do we kiss, do we weep, do we swear we are against the world? What? What?

'Everything'll be all right, a doddle, don't worry . . .', he said and pulled away from her.

'Frank, when will you come to Amsterdam . . .?'

But he shrugged at her worries and retreated, waving to her over the tourists' heads.

'Have a holiday with Elsa . . .', he said.

Oh yes, Cecily thought, bitterly. I need a holiday to get over this holiday.

Then she found herself, numbed, strapped into an aeroplane with Elsa's slim legs in immaculately pumiced jeans crossed beside her.

Trapped in flight.

She wanted to get off the plane. She wanted to baulk. Even as it taxied to the runway, she wanted to unstrap herself and run to the cockpit, shouting for them to allow her to get off.

Where am I being taken, where am I being delivered? The steel tube of the aircraft's passenger cabin sloped upward. A group of Germans, twenty year-olds in sun-hats, cheered and began to open their duty-free bottles. The glory of the upper atmosphere, the blazing blue, increased her panic and her claustrophobia. The headrest of the seat before her was dirty. Was that a smear of choc-olate?

Tied up tight, parcelled up? Delivered to Amsterdam? Why were they going on by train to Amsterdam from Cologne? So as not to be followed? To try to shake off Peter Carter? Parcelled . . . Was she to be dumped in a railway station left-luggage room, in brown paper and string, a ticket on her ankle, until it suited Frank to col-lect?

The double whisky miniature and ginger ale she ordered from the drinks trolley did not settle her. Elsa unnerved her. Was she content to be a talking centrefold, bland and bright, heavily scented? This tinsel girl with her perfect legs and little leather bolero jacket, her black, shiny vanity bag beneath the seat beside her black stiletto heels, in a halo of scent, was she to be her keeper?

Elsa tried to make conversation on the flight.

'You are diving?' she said.

'Sorry?'

'I am scuba diving.'

'Oh, no, I've never done that.'

'I am.'

'Ah.'

'But not for seeing fishes. I am wreck diving. The wrecks of ships.'

Not for a moment did Cecily believe this. It's a line, she thought. Elsa shoots it to her clients, without a doubt. The spinning of stories, the promises of silk and glamour, of flying around the world into a never-ending, glorious sunset, thirty thousand feet up in the deep blue sky, whisky forever in your hand . . . All lies. The promises of professional fantasists.

She closed her eyes. Images, pale and pink, near to dreams, swam before her. She was lying, naked, her body gigantic, on a sleeping bag on the hard floor of a huge airport. It was deserted. Grass grew along the cracks of the huge concrete slabs of the floor. A Greek, in traditional costume, like one of the many dolls seen in the tourist shops, a floppy cap, a white skirt. The doll-man was sweeping the airport's floor. 'No flight, no flight,' a painted mouth on a wooden head was saying.

And she woke with a start.

The plane was into its descent to Cologne airport. The young Germans had become sleepy, now only the odd surly growl came from them. A stewardess was leaning over her, her tray was down . . .

And then, a little miracle happened.

'Entschuldigen Sie mir, bitte. Wie commt man vom Flughafen an den Hauptbahnhof? Elsa said to the stewardess.

Cecily's German was excellent, from her schooling in Switzerland. Now it unlocked, like opening up a room she had not been in for years to find everything perfect, the ornaments on the mantel shelf untouched, a clock that only needed winding up. The room was where she could meet Elsa and get to know her.

In her own language, Elsa was a different young

woman. She was Dutch, from the German-speaking area near Arnhem, and not at all the beach icon Cecily had known in Crete. She was lively and quick witted, playful, even schoolgirlish.

She laughed and dug Cecily in the ribs when she realised they had German in common.

'I wanted to talk to you, my sweet, all along!' she said, her accent tinged with Northern German idiom. 'But English is a nightmare. Like Englishmen. Tongue-tied. Not your Frank though,' she added. 'He is a gentleman.'

'Is he?' said Cecily.

Elsa shot her a glance. 'Yeah, I really will talk to you,' she said. 'You've been playing a dangerous game with that one . . .'

So, all the time that Elsa, dumb-blonde, bikini-clad Elsa, had been with them, she had watched and judged, she had known. Cecily was wide awake now. A joy flooded her. She had had an ally without realising it.

Elsa had asked the stewardess about the railway station because she did not want to take a taxi. This parsimoniousness was typical of her. They took a transit bus. They were hungry, but Elsa would not buy food on the railway station. 'Kraut muck,' she said, fooling Cecily with the phrase for a moment. 'We'll get out own.' Though she was born into their language, Elsa did not like the Germans at all.

In Cologne city centre, Elsa found a bakery and bought rolls, then led Cecily quickly into and out of a small supermarket. She bought a tub of sauerkraut. In the square before the cathedral she produced a small sausage and a jar of gherkins from inside her coat. Cecily felt a frisson of fright. She had not had the slightest inkling in the supermarket that Elsa was stealing. It was the expertise with which it had been done, as much as the theft itself, which frightened her.

'Does stealing bother you?' asked Elsa.

'No,' she said uncertainly.

'I say, taking anything you can from the Germans. After what they took from us.'

They shared the bought and the stolen food, chewing big mouthfuls in the open air. To Cecily the garlicky, coarse meat of the sausage tasted sweet. A stolen German sausage? How could that give her hope that a kind of mad freedom may yet be possible? But it did, standing there chewing in a dire, grim city.

The dash for freedom, the escapade of her marriage, the confused months with Frank, perhaps it was not yet done.

The two women behaved like teenagers, giggling, standing there licking their fingers. Above them rose the huge, blackened bulk of Cologne Cathedral, the railway station nestling at its side, so close it seemed that you could catch a train from the transept inside. Cecily looked up. The dark towers curved against the sky, they made her dizzy. For a moment the food stuck in her throat. She swallowed, determindly.

'I don't like you,' she said to the cathedral.

'That's right,' said Elsa. 'You tell it.'

'Go on, say something,' Cecily said to the mighty building. 'Tell me what big towers you've got.'

Cologne Cathedral deigned not to reply.

It did not say, I am the state, I am history, I am not even aware you are below me, tiny in my shadow, and now I am going to fall on you. That's what you want to say, you bastard, isn't it, she thought. Or is there something in this sauerkraut making me lose my mind?

Elsa laughed. 'Turn round. Go on, turn round.'

She did. Before her there was a fast-food restaurant, shops, a shopping precinct, benches, a few sick-looking trees with an air of urban blight about them. With the gigantic cathedral at her back and out of sight, the scene could have been anywhere, Swindon, Slough, any mediocre town in Northern Europe.

'See?' said Elsa. 'It's not really there.'

'Let's see.'

They stood hand in hand, looking at the shops. Then they turned quickly together. They tried it again and again, laughing, becoming dizzy, until at the twentieth or so time of turning, for a bewildering split second, just for a moment, she could have sworn that . . .

On the train to Amsterdam, as it hummed and rattled into dying light toward the Dutch border, past endless flat fields, Cecily and Elsa sat together in the restaurant car. There were few passengers. The yellow tassels of the table lamps, the edges to the red tablecloths, swayed to the train's movement. Elsa drank spa water, Cecily beer, which was making her sleepy.

I am going over the border, she thought, 'over the border', the phrase repeating in her head like a half-remembered line from a pop song. Anywhere, nowhere, over the border in the secret train's tatty luxury, we, the empresses of the known world glide . . . So tired. She moved her chair nearer to Elsa and leant her head upon her shoulder.

What am I to do, in Amsterdam?

Elsa put her arm around her and said, as if she had been reading Cecily's thoughts about the train journey, the fantasy of being empresses in a private railway carriage, on their way to their execution, or members of the Tsar's family, rattling across the Russian steppes at night, locked in the train, moving towards a firing squad at dawn, 'Oh Cis. You are the older woman, but you're the romantic one.'

'Thank you, Miss,' said Cecily, and yawned, snug against Elsa's shoulder. Then, pricked awake by Elsa's words, 'Do you really think so?'

'Oh yes, very much.' Elsa hesitated. 'Perhaps I should find you somewhere else to stay. You won't like my life.'

'No, I'll stay with you.'

'My life is not romantic.'

'I feel safe with you.'

'Nowhere is safe, my sweet,' said Elsa, matter-of-factly. Cecily raised her head and looked at her. The young woman's gaze was hard and steady.

Down the alley in the Red Light District came the English youths. 'Here we go here we go here we go,' they sang. Cecily saw them from the second-floor window of the old house. My compatriots, Cecily thought. My fellow Brits. The voices of my country, ignorant, braying. It was better now, the girls in the brothel told her, since they banned English football teams from Europe. But you still got the odd coach-load of surrogate football supporters, over for a weekend. Cecily knew the scene below, she didn't need to look down.

'Here we go, here we go, here we go . . .' Oh God, why can't the English sing? Every other nation, abroad, drinking, having a good time, can sing real songs. But the English? The mindless 'Here we go, here we go, here we go . . .' Foreigners must think that that is our national anthem. Perhaps it is, now. Cecily smiled. Here she was, living in a room in the upper storey of a brothel, feeling prissy and disapproving, like an outraged vicar's wife writing to the Daily Telegraph.

'Gor look at that . . .' Now, she knew, they were ogling

the whores standing in the windows on the ground floor. Was Elsa in a window at the moment? Yes, thought Cecily, I think she said she was going to do a couple of hours, early this evening. 'Gor, wouldn't touch that with a barge pole.' 'Go on Ken . . .' 'Yeah. Go on Ken . . .' 'Gor look at this one.' 'Gor, rough?' 'Gor.'

The youths fell silent. Cecily knew what was happening down in the alley. Elsa had beckoned to them, rolled her tongue, slipped her finger in her G-string. Now the big boys were backing away.

'Let's go and have a drink . . .' 'Yeah, fuck . . .' 'C'mon.' And they were moving away down the alley, getting the chant going again to recover the dent in their collective manhood.

They didn't like the English in the brothels. They put the real punters off, the middle-aged men on their own, lonely and dreaming before the window whores. The clients had to be enticed within skilfully, with a sudden smile from the naked woman behind the glass, a sudden gesture.

Cecily sank into the faded chintz armchair beside her single bed. The only other furniture was a small fridge, to keep cold beers in. It was a small room in the old house of many rooms. The walls were wooden, partitions which, long ago, had been put in to break up a grander room.

Who had sat here at these windows in the seventeenth century, she thought. The wife of a merchant, an embroidery frame before her, children with curls at her knees, like you saw in the interminable rows of paintings in the Rijksmuseum? What would she have made of these cupboards in her grand house, cupboards occupied by girls resting from their dreary trade below, in one cupboard me, the wife of a foreign criminal, hiding?

This is the death of romance, she thought, flipping

open the top of a Grolsch beer. I am drinking too much.
I've slept all day and will be up all night, doing nothing.
Nothing at all.

I am waiting, she told herself. This respectably sordid
city, with its dark houses and canals of dirty, deep brown
water, it's a crossroads. Here I sit. They will all come,
eventually, Frank and the others. I am doing nothing
because there is nothing I can do, but wait.

Elsa had shown her the brothel and the flat with its
armchair and fridge, she had introduced her to the girls
and the rather strange personnel who looked after the
girls, with a wary and off-handed manner. Only first
names were used. There were two middle-aged women,
identical twins, very short and fat, each with the same
front tooth missing. Their names were Beatrice and
Francesca. Dantesque fantasy names, that they had used
in their youth when they were whores? They washed
clothes, sewed sequins, hoovered the window rooms, they
cooked in a communal backroom. They were friendly to
Cecily, keeping the fridge stocked with beer, washing her
clothes, making sandwiches of crusty bread, cheese and
gherkins for her.

The only man she saw in the brothel, for she was
always shooed away from any chance encounter with a
customer from the street, was a man called Billy. He
wore a suit and a trilby hat, which he did not take off. He
talked to Elsa in Dutch and said nothing to her. The
pimp of the house? Cecily could not tell.

On her arrival, Cecily had seen that Elsa feared it
would be too much for her, this world in the old house
that mixed homeliness and domesticity with the brutal
matter-of-factness of the twenty-pound-a-time tricks in
the window rooms at street level behind pulled curtains.
But she found herself at home amongst the ugliness

that disfigured the lanes, the tiny courtyards and the streets beside the narrow canals, the area violet at night, deep violet despite the red lights and the strobes that flashed from open doorways to the rhythm of rock music. The reduction of desire to this blatant trade comforted her. Walking one evening she had looked up at the tall windows of a beautiful house the other side of a canal. In the window, in red light that flickered against a ceiling painted black, a naked girl was moving in slow motion to attract the punters, a dance, her frail arms rising in slow motion above her head. It was beautiful, it was crass. The fantasy in the window far outstripped what was on offer, she knew. That was what she liked. This was the best place in the world for someone in love to hide.

She soon realised that there was a hierarchy in the area, that there were three circles in this degradation. They were at odds with each other. The first two circles were amongst the window whores in the brothels, a simple division between those who were addicts and those who were not. It was drugs that drew the geography here. Sooner or later, usually a year, Elsa told her, a whore on drugs found her looks going and lost her place in the windows. There was a limit to the 'centrefold' illusion that could be maintained by a lace corset and red gelatine across a couple of light bulbs. Elsa told her of Pauline, of whom they had been very fond. They had tried to protect her, but, said Elsa, 'it was always hopeless.' She had gone 'out'.

'Out', that is down to the third circle, on the streets with the drug whores, selling a trick for five guilders, not using condoms, trading without pimps, beaten up by the pushers. At first, Cecily had not seen this shadow-life in the streets. When Elsa pointed it out to her, she saw it everywhere. The pushers stood on the bridge where the

211

real Red Light District began, like sentinels, their hands in their pockets, silent, eyeing the crowds of sightseers and potential clients as they walked, unknowingly, into the pushers' domain. The violence in the area was from the uneasy frontier between the brothels and the streets. No street plan explained this dangerous geography. Elsa's world saw the drug whores and their pushers as a threat, she said they were destroying the area. They threatened its mythical status of being 'clean' and 'safe' for the punters, its anti-septic dream.

Most of the girls were now from the Far East. Elsa was a rarity, a Dutch country whore. At her invitation, Cecily had watched her with a customer, through a peep-hole from the back room. Beside a washing-machine that Beatrice and Francesca used for the establishment's sheets, satin corsets and panties, as well as everyday clothes, Cecily stood with her eye to the wall. What she witnessed was more of a medical examination than a satyric episode, 'Man with a Maid'. Fifteen minutes, twenty pounds, another ten as a tip, a slow Scandinavian. 'You give them a good look over,' Elsa explained later. 'One pimple and they are back outside.' Cecily saw Elsa be sweet but cool with the customer, she made passion impossible. She supplied the condom. She gave him a drink afterwards, and a dusting down with talcum powder, then out. The Scandinavian seemed relieved to go.

'See?' said Elsa, afterwards, 'they are all boring.' They sat drinking mugs of china tea in Elsa's cupboard room. In a corner there was scuba diving equipment and a wet suit, hung above a diving bag. Elsa really did dive to wrecks.

Having just seen her at work, Cecily was shocked that this beautiful, athletic young woman 'went to the windows'. She had thought, when their friendship began

before Cologne Cathedral, that Elsa would in some way
be special, have a special clientele, that she would not be
so degraded. 'I expected . . .', she began and hesitated. 'I
thought it would be special.'

Elsa sipped her tea and shrugged. 'Whoring is whoring.
And the windows are cleaner.'

'Cleaner?'

'Cleaner than going to hotels. There are pigs in the
hotels, and you're alone. You can get men who go crazy.
The johns here are harmless, you're in control. There are
people near, if you get a madman.'

'Why do you do it?' Again, she hesitated. 'Sorry, I don't
mean to offend . . .'

'No offence,' said Elsa. 'Straight people always ask. But
you'll never get an answer, Cis. Not even from me. The
johns often ask, the shy ones. I say I'm a student, doing it
for a year. Or a housewife. They like that.'

She walked to the window of her cupboard, the mug of
tea in her hand. A Snoopy mug. Elsa's room was at the
back of the house, overlooking a courtyard. Cecily looked
down. Below the scene could have been a Vermeer painting, there was an archway of red bricks and white mortar,
and a woman was sweeping the courtyard, though in a
leather miniskirt and high heels, not seventeenth-century
apron and clogs.

'The truth is . . .', said Elsa, 'you cross over. You go
through a mirror. Everything's the other way round, sex,
love. And you never get back through.' She shrugged.
'But you know all about it.'

'Do I?'

'With Frank.'

I have crossed over. She sipped her tea. Crossed over
the crossroads. She decided to go out, as she decided to do
every evening.

How long have I drifted like this? Only three weeks? In a mirror in a bar, she would see that she was attaining the look of one of Amsterdam's wastrels. Not derelicts or vagrants, but people, mainly foreigners, who seemed to be doing nothing, crawling the cafés and coffee shops. Her skin was white, her eyes were tired. Am I going to seed, in this indifferent city?

The area was working its way into the evening. The best hours for the trade were yet to come, they were between midnight and two in the morning, when drink loosened wallets. The sex shops, which always seemed empty, blazed with the crude colour of their magazine covers. Crowds slewed about, the shuffling of their feet echoed between the houses. The girls in the windows, standing all but naked, seemed strangely disguised by the strips of lace about their thighs.

She walked with no purpose, crossing the Dam Square to the City's more respectable side.

Where am I now? Traffic. The Rozengracht. A sign above some kind of club, 'Frau Holle'. Have I been in there? Traipsing round the city for three weeks, she felt she had been in everywhere there was to waste time, to sit, to go to seed for a few more hours . . .

And she was sitting in a comfortable chair before a table, in a softly lit room. There were few people at the tables. Behind glass, as if in an aquarium, there was a theatre. On a platform stage there was a brightly lit model of a dinosaur, walking in the Grand Canyon. The dinosaur had a long neck and a human face.

Nothing was happening. Cecily ordered a glass of white wine from a waiter with long hair. She sipped.

Eveline was sitting at a table, alone, at the front, staring through the glass at the stage.

It was her. The cut of hair, short at the neck, the long

head, held high above narrow, upright shoulders.

No, no. She will get out of me why I'm here, she'll take one look at me and I will horrify her. Please no. Cecily began to panic.

Then a young man came into the café and went to Eveline's table. He leaned forward and kissed her neck. Eveline turned.

It wasn't her after all. Nothing like her, much younger, wearing lipstick. And sadness flooded into Cecily.

A second before she had been dreading it being Eveline. Now she could not bear it not being her.

If it had been you, in this strange place, staring at that dinosaur thing, that repellent thing on the stage?

No, no, Eveline, that's unfair, that's cruel . . . I made a dash for freedom. I did, I really did. I wanted to go down, deep down, and begin a new life, from the bottom.

Don't be so hard on me, what happened to you and Mary, after all? What new way of living did you invent?

The lights changed. A very young Chinese woman was on the stage, she was manipulating the dinosaur with puppet strings. A tape began to play. The head of the vile model turned toward Cecily and, on an intercom from the theatre behind the glass, said, in a bland, female American voice, 'It was such a fine day. So I went for a walk in the Garden of Eden. And a man driving a Chevrolet came along the highway . . .'

Cecily rose in revulsion, left some money, any money, on the table and stumbled from the club.

An hour, two hours later, she thought, how many bars have I crawled? It was getting late. She had made her way back across the city.

Go back to the room. Sleep. In the morning, do something about your hair.

Yes, Eveline.

Then, at the bridge where the pushers stood at the entrance to the Red Light District, she saw a man, limping. A drunk. Limping. It was Peter Carter.

The drink churned its nausea in her. I am seeing ghosts . . .

Amongst the crowds, now bold with the night's excitements, for the area's activities were at their height, she followed the limping black-coated figure.

Yes a night for ghosts. The man was talking to a scruffy, dangerous-looking young man outside a disco. Scoring? Cecily walked on, passing them.

No ghost. There was no doubt. It was Carter. He looked haggard and ill, his face a permanent grimace.

She tasted vomit in her mouth. She got back to the house. Clucking with concern, Beatrice and Francesca put her to bed.

Alive, or as ghosts, they were making their way to her.

Frank came three days later, days which had been dreadful. Who, on the street, was one of Carter's colleagues, or informers? Which bejeaned, scruffy young man, with his hands in a leather jacket, was 'one of them'? A walkytalky, a revolver, under the black leather? Are they observing me? As I crawl, bar to bar?

I thought I was safe. I thought I had the freedom, of this of all places, to hide and be in love.

A delusion. 'Nowhere is safe,' Elsa had said, on the train from Cologne, bringing me here.

She tried to dry out. She was juddered, there was a flickering tremble in her fingers that she could do nothing about.

I am living in a small hut, she thought, on the edge of the first circle of hell. She saw the image with the power of an hallucination. A small hut, a meadow slopes away from my door, below there is a bottomless valley. Up the lawn, they will come crawling, hideous things, small dinosaurs the size of dogs, with human voices. On one of them, Peter Carter, riding.

She decided to give up the attempt to stop drinking. She went to a bar round the corner from the brothel. It was a traditional Dutch pub, local people drank quietly there. It seemed invisible to the punters and the roaring English louts. She looked across the scrubbed, worn, wooden table at herself in a large mirror on the wall.

The Amsterdam wastrel looked back. Paint me like this, she thought. That woman over there, sitting alone, who was once in love. And Elsa was in the mirror, holding open the door of the bar. 'Frank is here,' she said.

Up and up the twisting red carpet of the narrow staircase she ran. Up and up, to her room.

He was leaning over the opened fridge, a bottle of beer in his hand.

'Greatest beer in the world,' he said. And grinned. And then he was on his knees, exhausted, weeping.

She got him out of his clothes, which smelt with days of sweat and travel, and into a bath. He talked and talked, he kept grabbing her arms to make her listen. She wanted, madly, to lather him with soap, to scrub him all over, to wash away the panic that he reeked of. But he kept on trying to hold her, like a madman, condemned to tell his story, over and over again, its incidents jumbled in any order.

'No, no Frank . . . It's all right . . .'

But he went on and on, after she had got him out of the bath, back into her room. He pulled blankets about him, he sat on the floor sucking at beer bottles, he crammed the sandwiches Beatrice and Francesca had brought up to them, their eyes alight with interest.

'I got to the ship . . . Lights all over, fog. Light in the

fog. The fucking ship, it looked like a magic castle. Dun Laoghaire. Didn't believe I'd get that far. Holyhead, the train, right across the country, Harwich ferry . . . I walked through 'em. You could feel them everywhere. I just walked through them, eh? Like the Devil having all the luck, eh? The Devil being like Jesus, walking all the way across the fucking North Sea . . .'

No Frank, thought Cecily, unable to get near him because of the wildness of his movements. They didn't arrest you because they wanted you to get here, to Amsterdam, and Peter Carter. What would they say at your trial? She understood the deadening truth of his wild flight. They will let Peter Carter shoot you, to save them embarrassment.

On poured the fractured narrative. She could do nothing to stop it.

'We were set up, we were going to hit a van . . . An ambush. But we were set up. The Provos set us up, left us to it. The Garda knew we were coming, they were waiting for us Cis. Me and Brian, they dumped us . . . They got Brian, Cis.'

And the look in his eyes was of someone reduced, forever.

'I held him in my arms. There wasn't a mark on him. I couldn't see where they'd got him, at first. Then I moved my hand from under his head, and I . . .'

He was suddenly calm. He paused, looking at Cecily. His eyes were pale, as it there was nothing behind them at all.

'I held his brains in my hand. I was holding my brother's brains, y'know what I thought?' He laughed. He was telling her this evenly. 'I thought what the hell, Brian old son, there was never much grey matter there at the best of times. Spread it about, why not? Spread it all over fucking Ireland.'

At last she could hold him, as he curled up in his uncontrollable weeping.

And, a little later, they lay in the single bed. She held his head, she swept his hair back again and again, he was hot, drenched in sweat, fits of trembling came in waves, his limbs were rigid. She smoothed herself over him. They were naked and tight together in the small bed, she smoothed the length of his body. And, slowly she was able to weaken him, to kneed the tension from him, and they made love, wrapped together, he holding her so tight it was as if they were struggling to breathe from the same pair of lungs.

Yet, all the time, removed from their passion, Cecily's thoughts ran cold and clear and calm.

We are quite dead now, she thought. And it is all worthwhile. It is worth more than anything else I could imagine.

She held him, her hand in the small of his back. Their lovemaking's tide ebbed. A window was half open. Outside the noise of the rock music, the shouts in the streets, were fading. It began to rain, gently. A coolness came into the room.

'You and me in this hole,' he said. 'They looked after you? You not had any aggro . . . ?'

'No. They like me. I'm in love, you see.'

'What a place for it.'

'Any place will do,' she said.

He smiled. 'It was you that brought the dirty mind to this marriage, I do believe,' he said.

She felt them both going limp, into sleep.

'You and me. Yeah. You and me. We can walk over the water, through walls.'

He was asleep before her. She lay, looking at the drops of rain accumulating on the windows.

And woke. Frank was not there. It was light. She

219

looked at her watch. Six o'clock. But morning, evening? She put on a kimono robe that belonged to Elsa and rushed down the stairs. There was a smell of bacon and eggs.

And in the back room with the gas stove and the washing-machine, there was Frank, fit and fresh.

'I don't understand about the Dutch 'n' bacon,' he said, frying pan in hand. 'It's all this ham, this pearly smoked stuff. Hello doll.' He gave her a peck on the cheek.

Elsa sat there, a trenchcoat about her, smoking. 'Frank is at breakfast but it is dinner time,' she said in her broken English.

'You slept all day. Getting a bit of a slag, doll?' He laughed. 'Picking up the local customs?'

'You are rude,' said Elsa.

Cecily felt a panic rising in her, and a fury at him. I haven't told him, who I saw, in the street . . . Near here, three days ago. But she heard herself say, 'You feel better?'

'A million dollars,' he said. 'Want breakfast?'

'No.'

But he ignored her. He turned to Elsa. 'Els', where is Billy? Listen. Billy, I want Billy.'

'Billy is coming,' said Elsa.

'He better be,' said Frank, slapping eggs, bacon and fried bread onto a plate, then perching on the arm of Elsa's chair to eat, fork in hand. 'You meet Billy while you've been here?'

Billy? There was a man, with a trilby hat, she remembered.

'No,' said Elsa, forestalling her.

'Glad to hear it. Don't want that slime near my old lady.'

Why don't I say they are out there, he is out there? She

felt her mouth tighten, she was frightened that she would not be able to stand there a second longer, that she would fall to the ground.

'Who's Billy?' she heard herself ask.

'Billy? Business partner, in't he? He pimps this place for me.' He paused, looking down at his plate. 'For me and Brian, that is.' He raised a whole egg to his mouth.

So he hadn't told Elsa of Brian's death? And . . .

'For you? You run this place?'

' 'Course,' egg on his lip. 'Bit of an absent landlord. Been a major investment over the years. Billy looked after it for me, while I was inside. Time to cash up and get out.'

She stared at him. As if to explain something obvious he said, 'He's Colombian, in't he? The Colombians are big in Amsterdam. You've got to be in with 'em, if you're going to hang onto anything round here.'

She backed away.

'I will work,' said Elsa, standing, taking off the trenchcoat. 'It is six o'clock, I will do an hour.' She was standing in the room, all but naked. Cecily looked at Elsa's skin, it was covered with pink powder, subduing her suntan. Picks up the coloured light, I see, thought Cecily, her thoughts mechanical. The room filled with the cloying powder's scent. But it had always been there, she realised, that awful smell . . .

'Yeah, do that Els',' said Frank, brusquely, looking at Cecily.

'It's all right,' said Elsa, painted, powdered, naked but wholly disguised, a lisp in her voice that Cecily had not heard before. 'Frank will take you away, you will be safe.'

She went. Frank rested the plate on the arm of the chair.

Now tell him. Tell him, tell him, warn him!

'Billy will get us to Rio,' he said.

Rio? The name of a city, but totally unreal, a word without a place.

Warn him!

'The world's not as tight as the bastards think,' Frank was saying. 'Shitheads and crazies, real crazies like me and you, we can still slip through.'

And he burst into tears. They streamed down his face. She went to him and they kissed.

Her thoughts were, as they had been in the night, cold and calm, running apart from her.

I don't want to tell him. What if we escaped, what if we found ourselves in another city, half the world away? It would only delay what is coming a few months, a few years. We're perfect now. Quite perfect.

I won't tell him. She put her hands to his face and kissed him deeply. Their embrace was an exchange of equals, two people, wholly free with each other. We had that as lovers, she thought. That we did have. We are, briefly, free with each other.

From the front of the house there was a cry. Frank ran to the spy-hole in the wall. He turned and leant against the wall, looking at Cecily. She knew at once.

'Used the postcard, did you Doll? Rang the bastard after all? Tipped him off I was coming?'

'No,' she said.

'It don't matter, love. It don't matter at all,' and he smiled.

And Peter Carter came into the room, the door opening, a door of faded cream paint, once a beautiful door, she thought, moulded. She didn't look at Carter, black in the door frame, at an angle, she looked at Frank, who was smiling.

'It's a doddle,' she said.

222

Peter Carter's machine pistol fired so quickly, that their deaths were virtually simultaneous.

Elsa led Matty into the backroom.

'You are the sister?' said this woman, this creature, for the third time. 'It is the room.'

'Oh this wretched place.'

'The police have gone away now,' the woman said. 'I am not clearing yet. I am sorry.'

'No, please,' said Matty. 'I just wanted to see . . .' See where my sister and her husband died, I had to bring myself to, I should not have, thought Matty, managing to add, 'Please don't worry.'

'I do not clear it. The German newspapers come to photograph this afternoon.'

'Ah.'

'You are the sister?'

Yes I am the sister, Matty wanted to scream, yes, yes!

'Not to be sad,' Elsa said. 'They had much fun.'

Matty could not bear the sudden tenderness in the lisping voice. She was about to weep, uncontrollably. 'I . . .', but she could say nothing.

'Much fun,' said Elsa. 'Romantisch. They were romantic.'